Advanced
TURKEY HUNTING

BY Michael Hanback

CREATIVE
PUBLISHING
international

CHANHASSEN, MINNESOTA

www.creativepub.com

MICHAEL HANBACK has been chasing wild turkeys and trophy whitetails in many states and provinces for more than 25 years, and he's become a nationally acclaimed hunting expert.

He is contributing editor for *Turkey & Turkey Hunting* and *Whitetail Hunting Strategies.* He is also a field editor and columnist for *Outdoor Life* and the National Rifle Association's *American Hunter* magazine. Hanback has authored several books, including the acclaimed *Spring Gobbler Fever.* He appears on many hunting videos and television programs each year.

He lives in Virginia with his wife and two sons.

CREATIVE PUBLISHING international

Copyright © 2003 by Creative Publishing international, Inc.
18705 Lake Drive East
Chanhassen, MN 55317
1-800-328-3895
www.creativepub.com

President/CEO: Michael Eleftheriou

Vice President/Publisher: Linda Ball

Vice President/Retail Sales & Marketing: Kevin Haas

Executive Editor, Outdoor Group: Barbara Harold

Creative Director: Brad Springer

Photo Editor and Project Manager: Angela Hartwell

Director, Production Services: Kim Gerber

Production Manager: Helga Thielen

Production Staff: Laura Hokkanen, Stephanie Barakos

Printed on American paper by: R. R. Donnelley
10 9 8 7 6 5 4 3 2 1

ADVANCED TURKEY HUNTING
by Michael Hanback

Cover Photo: Gary Kramer

Contributing Photographers: Jon Blumb, Kathy Butt, Tim Christie, Soc Clay, Michael H. Francis, John Hafner, Brad Herndon, Tes Randle Jolly, Donald M. Jones, Brian Kenney, Gary Kramer, Bill Marchel, John E. Phillips, Len Rue Jr., Dusan Smetana

Contributing Individuals: Ray Eye, Jay Gregory, Terry Drury, Steve Stoltz, Ronnie Strickland

Contributing Manufacturers: Hunter Specialties, Knight & Hale Game Calls, M.A.D. Calls, Primos Hunting Calls, Quaker Boy Game Calls, Realtree Camouflage

Library of Congress Cataloging-in-Publication Data

Hanback, Michael.
    Advanced turkey hunting: turkey hunting's top experts reveal their secrets for success / by Michael Hanback.
        p. cm. – (The complete hunter)
        ISBN 1-58923-064-7
        1. Turkey hunting. I. Title. II. Complete hunter (Creative Publishing International)

SK325.T8 H34 2003
799.2'4645--dc21   2002035037

CONTENTS

Introduction

Are you new to wild turkey hunting? Or are you a seasoned veteran who has tagged your share of long-bearded toms? Well, it does not matter. This book, which features the expertise of 20 pros with a combined 500 years of turkey-hunting wisdom, will teach you a lot. A whole lot.

Advanced Turkey Hunting goes way beyond the basics of this scintillating sport. Missouri pro Mark Drury doesn't just tell you how to roost a gobbler on a spring evening; he instructs how to climb into bed with a turkey (well, almost!). Alabaman Eddie Salter explains that calling and "working" an old tom are two entirely different things; once you understand that, you'll dupe more birds. Kentucky pro Harold Knight breaks the wild turkey's spring breeding season into five distinct phases, and offers specific hunting and calling tactics for each period.

That's just a sampling of the great stuff you'll find in this book. Seventeen other chapters offer in-depth advice on all aspects of turkey hunting, from super scouting, to finding gobbler flocks in the fall, to beating the crowds on public land, to closing the deal when a gobbler struts inside bow or shotgun range. While much of the information is geared toward hunting and calling the widespread Eastern wild turkey, there are also focused chapters and sections of text that deal with the intricacies of hunting the Osceola, or Florida, subspecies, as well as the Rio Grande and Merriam's subspecies out West. It's all here!

When you camo up and hit the woods in either spring or fall, think back to this book from time to time. Remember, you are drawing upon 500 years of turkey-hunting wisdom! Size up each hunting situation, and give those gobblers the pros' best tricks—the ones you read right here. You can't help but score your share of beards and spurs.

Here's to many safe, fun and memorable mornings in the turkey woods.

Michael Hanback
Spring, 2003

LOCATING
GOBBLERS

LOCATING GOBBLERS

Super Scouting for Turkeys

with Michael Hanback

Your average hunter does his scouting a week or so before the start of the spring season. He heads out at dawn and listens for turkeys gobbling on the roost. As the sky blushes blue and pink, a tom roars from a nearby ridge or creek bottom. The guy pumps his fists and hollers, "I know where I'm gonna be on opening day!" His scouting is pretty much done.

Well, news flash: Just because a turkey picked that spot to gobble his fool head off doesn't mean you can expect to waltz in on opening morning, stroke a few yelps on a box call, and shoot the big bird. Far from it! Too many things can and will go wrong.

After he flies down, the turkey may choose to head away from where you're set up (there's a 50-50 chance). A ditch or creek you don't know about might hang up the gobbler and keep him from coming to your calls. Or another hunter might walk in on you, hooting, yelping and messing things up. Yikes!

Well, here's another news flash: You can alleviate those problems and others by taking your scouting to a higher level.

It's a two-part process. First, get off the couch and hike your hunt zones a month or so before the season. Then, as opening day nears, drive and walk around and listen for gobbles as you always have. Ah, but when a tom bellows at dawn, don't leave. Hang in the woods for an hour or longer, listening

The Expert: **Michael Hanback** has been hunting and writing about wild turkeys for 25 years. Although he makes his home in Warrenton, Virginia, he's had the good fortune of traveling across the country and hunting with every one of the pros who contributed to this book. He says unequivocally, "These guys are the best turkey hunters in the world! They rule the woods, and their hunting and calling advice is sure to make you more successful." Before delving into the masters' plans, Hanback begins with a chapter on scouting—not any old scouting, but super scouting. "It lays the groundwork for scoring turkey beards and spurs," he says.

to the turkeys and patterning them. Where do the gobblers go to strut and tread hens after they fly down each morning? Where do the hens go to feed and nest? Are there other scouters in the area? Find out by taking your scouting a step further.

"Who has time for all that work?" you might ask. Well, it's really not a big deal. A few days of super scouting, and you will locate more than a few toms to hunt.

Gaining the Terrain Advantage

Spend a few days roaming a private or public hunting ground with a topographical map and/or an aerial photograph in hand. (A good source for maps is www.usgs.gov on the Internet.) Get a little exercise while you scout for turkey tracks, scratchings, feathers and droppings. (See the sidebar "Turkey Sign.")

If you are like most of America's 2.6 million turkey hunters, you go for Eastern wild turkeys. Studies show that in areas where food sources and

roost trees remain the same from year to year, flocks of this subspecies roam only 3,000 acres or so throughout the year. If you find loads of fresh sign on a property in, say, late February or early March, some toms will be gobbling there come opening day. The same holds true for the Osceola subspecies.

You might have to revise your thinking a bit if you hunt Rio Grande or Merriam's turkeys. Western birds sometimes travel miles each day between roosts, feeding areas, water holes and strut zones. (See the chapter "Vagabonds of the West" for details.)

Many scouts are so focused on spotting feathers, scat and the like that they miss the most reliable sign of all—two three-toed tracks with a longbeard standing in them! I never walk the woods without an 8X or 10X binocular slung around my neck. I glass pastures, food plots, old burns and similar openings. I check the sides and tops of ridges. After cresting hills, I aim my optic down into hollows and creek bottoms. It's easier than you think to slip around and spot turkeys.

Get out and scout your hunting areas before the spring season. Mark roost sites, feeding areas and any turkey sign you find on an aerial photo or topo map.

Here's a refresher course on the signs of turkey activity to be on the lookout for:

• **Tracks:** Scout for fresh tracks in fields, burns and old roadbeds; around creeks, stock tanks and other water sources; and anywhere the soil is bare, muddy or sandy. If the middle toe of a track is more than 2 inches long you're on the trail of a tom. Hen prints are noticeably shorter and smaller than gobbler tracks.

• **Strut Marks:** Check for narrow grooves in dirt or sand on either side of large tracks—that's where a gobbler scraped his wing feathers on the ground as he strutted around. Lots of strut marks—especially in a dusty roadbed or sandy creek bottom—might tip you off to a hen-gathering zone that a tom visits most every day.

• **Droppings:** A field edge, oak flat, logging road or similar feeding area or travel lane is a good place to find droppings. Gobbler scat is big and shaped like a fishhook. Hen droppings are small, round and spiraled. In spring, fresh scat is moist, green and splashed with white; in fall, when hens and toms feed heavily on mast, it is brown and dry.

• **Feathers:** Did you know 5,000 to 6,000 feathers cover an adult turkey's body? Hens and gobblers lose some of those feathers when flying down from the roost, preening or fighting. Find a long, white-barred wing feather with a square, rubbed tip, and you know a gobbler once strutted in the area. Look for the small, black-tipped breast feathers that only toms have.

• **Dust Bowls:** Scout for shallow bowls or "wallows" on the edges of fields and in roadbeds. These indentations are the work of turkeys taking dust baths to repel mites. Lots of dust bowls may indicate a hen-nesting area; gobblers should strut nearby.

• **Scratchings:** When you're in the woods, keep an eye out for round, jagged ovals of upturned leaves, especially near trees and fallen logs. These scratches are made by turkeys raking for old mast, green shoots, insects and other food. In fall, winter and early spring, a "rolled up" ridge or flat tells you that turkeys are still traveling in big flocks. Later in the spring, pockets of fresh scratchings indicate that the birds have broken up and are traveling alone or in small breeding flocks. The larger the oval of upturned leaves, the better the odds that a gobbler scratched there.

Know your turkey subspecies and their habitat. These Merriam's will range farther than their Eastern counterparts each day, so factor that into your scouting.

QUICK TIP

◆◆◆◆◆◆◆◆

Keep an eye peeled for turkeys as you hunt deer. Say you're sitting in a tree stand one October day and hear a flock of birds scratching and calling 200 yards away. Glass the turkeys and sex them. If it's a gang of longbeards, great! Come April, a few of those toms will have dispersed a mile or farther, but many of them will be gobbling and strutting around the same woods.

◆◆◆◆◆◆◆◆

As far as terrain scouting goes, I've saved the best for last. As you snoop for sign and glass for birds, study the lay of the land. The best time to do this is from late February through early April, before the bulk of the spring green-up. The woods are barren and open, the color of copper in the East and South and silver-hued in the Midwest. It's a good time to look for maneuvering routes and calling spots. Here's what you should be looking for:

• Zero in on tall trees on points, knolls, bluffs and hillsides—they're prime places for toms to roost. Note ridge tops, flats, old logging roads and similar openings where birds might fly down and strut.

• Check out hollows, creek bottoms and ditches that will cover your moves as you slip close to gobbling birds.

• Scan the woods for fences, gullies, creeks and other obstacles that might hang up toms you call to. If you know where these hazards are, you can take them into account as you hunt.

• Get serious and look for specific trees—for example, a couple of big

white oaks on a scratched-up flat near a prime roosting site—where you might sit and yelp to a gobbler in a few weeks.

As you make your rounds, mark these prominent terrain features on your maps. The data will prove invaluable when it comes time to hunt.

Learning the Language of Love

One March afternoon, I walked a farm near my home in Virginia. Two miles into a rather uneventful hike, a crow cawed. Talk about a picker-upper—a tom shock-gobbled 200 yards away!

Wild turkeys are pretty vocal in late winter and early spring. As hens and gobblers establish pecking orders prior to mating, you're apt to hear yelping, cutting, aggravated purring (the call of two sparring toms) and maybe even sporadic gobbling. Hear the latter on a warm, sunny day, and you can bet a gang of toms inhabits the area. Chances are some of those birds will gobble and strut nearby when you come back to hunt in a few weeks.

By the way, I returned to that Virginia farm a month later, on opening morning of hunting season. A 22-pound tom with a thick beard and 1-inch spurs came to my clucks and yelps. Was it the same bird that shock-gobbled during my earlier scouting run? Who knows, and who cares? I scored!

In many parts of the country the first of two "gobbling peaks" occurs during the preseason in early March or around the first of April. In the frenzied process of gathering hens, toms gobble hard on the roost, fly down and gobble some more while strutting toward fields, oak flats and similar areas where hens feed and mingle.

As you're scouting, monitor those ground gobbles. Don't move in too tight on the toms, but stay within earshot. You might do a little owl-hooting or crow-calling to shock a few more gobbles from the birds, but don't use hen calls. Save your sexy clucks and yelps for opening day. Your goal now is to track the movements of the turkeys. You want to know as precisely as possible where toms roost, strut and breed. If you can pattern a walking, talking gobbler two or three mornings in a row, you should be pumped, because you've gone a long way toward tricking him.

Reaping the Fruits of Your Labor

Okay, opening day finally rolls around. On cue, 15 minutes before daybreak, a gobbler roars. Think back to your scouting. Sneak to a ridge or flat between the tom's roost tree and strut corridor. Circle to take a gully or creek out of play if you need to. Keep reading the terrain and fine-tuning things until you set up in a nice, open spot within 125 yards or so of the tom. You're now in great position to call in and whack that turkey.

It's opening morning, and the tom hasn't been called to or hassled by hunters for months. He's probably gobbling pretty well, hoping to attract hens. (Even if an old boy has a couple of girls, he always lusts for more.) You're set up in the gobbler's travel corridor and near his strut zone. I can think of no better scenario for him to come and check you out.

Don't yelp too much too early. Try a little seductive clucking and yelping instead. If things pan out and you tote home a fat tom with a long beard, chalk it up to super scouting.

SCOUT YOUR COMPETITION

As you scout for gobbling turkeys, look and listen for other hunters, especially on public land. Let's say it's three days before the spring opener and you locate a couple of birds bellowing on a ridge. But you also see two trucks parked nearby, and hear guys hooting and crow-calling. It's a no-brainer. Those other hunters will be on those toms the first day of the season.

Now is the time to get mobile and explore other options. The next morning, put some distance between you and those hunters. If you're scouting on a farm or woodland, drive to the opposite end. Or head to a more remote ridge or hollow in a national forest or state area.

Spend your scouting days trying to find a couple of turkeys that gobble in spots out of sight, mind and earshot of other people. It's always more fun—not to mention a lot safer—to hunt and call to a gobbler you have to yourself.

LOCATING GOBBLERS

Terrain Tactics for Hunters

with David Hale

There are three major types of turkey habitat across the United States: mountains and hills; open fields or plains; and swamplands. To score beards and spurs consistently, turkey pro David Hale has this advice: First, understand the behavior of toms in each of these habitats; and then tailor your hunting and calling strategies to the terrain.

Mountain Turkeys

In mountainous or hilly terrain, a gobbler usually likes to roost high in a hardwood tree on a ridge, on a point or a little way down the side of a slope. At first light, a tom stands up there with his claws wrapped around a limb and gobbles long and loud to attract hens. On a cold, rainy morning, a turkey might roost in a pine or hardwood tree a third to halfway down a slope, where he is sheltered and out of the wind. Later in the spring season, some toms roost farther down mountains and ridges so they can be closer to hens that nest around fields and in bottoms.

Wherever he roosts, a gobbler can see far and well as the pewter dawn breaks. So Hale and I have come up with our Three Golden Rules for mountain birds.

1. Never approach a turkey from below. As you huff and puff up a slope he'll look down and bust you. Always stick to the high ground and sneak toward him. "The walking will be easier and quieter, and there's less chance a gobbler will see you," says Hale.

The Expert: **David Hale** of Cadiz, Kentucky, has hunted all the subspecies of wild turkeys many times during the past three decades. Hale, co-founder of Knight & Hale Game Calls, is adamant when he says, "Turkey hunters put way too much emphasis on calling. Wherever you hunt, knowing your way around the woods is most important." You'd do well to practice what this pro preaches.

2. Set up on the same ridge or in the same draw with the turkey. If you're standing on a ridge and a bird gobbles on the next ridge or in a hollow a couple hundred yards away, hustle over there. Once in a blue moon, you can call a red-hot tom off a ridge, across a draw and up the next slope where you're set up. But it is always best to maneuver around and get on the same ridge or in the same hollow with a turkey. "The easier you make it for a gobbler to work to your calls, the better your chances of getting him," agrees Hale.

3. Always set up and call from a spot above a gobbler, or at least on the same level with him. Most mornings, a gobbler that roosts off a point or on a hillside will fly down to the "short side" of his tree. That is, he'll pitch 20 to 30 feet straight down to the hill rather than sailing 100 yards or farther into a hollow or bottom. "If you're set up 100 yards or so above the turkey or on the same level with him, you'll be in good position to call him in," says the Kentucky pro.

One April morning, Hale and I sneaked toward a hot-gobbling Tennessee turkey. Before we could set up, the old boy flew from his roost tree and alighted on the side of a ridge. Actually that worked to our advantage. We slipped in close and positioned ourselves in some open oaks above him. The tom roared for 30 minutes just over the lip of the ridge, sometimes honoring our yelps, sometimes simply gobbling on his own. I was tempted to move, but Hale whispered, "Sit still."

An hour later, here came the turkey, clumping up the ridge, white head gleaming in the sunlight. We got that tom not so much with calling as with patience.

In the spring, a longbeard roosts on a ridge or hillside for a couple of reasons. He can see well, so he feels safe up there. Also, it's a great way for a bird to gather hens first thing in the morning. Sometimes a turkey will pitch from his roost and travel over hill and dale, gobbling as he walks away. But most of the time, a tom will pitch out and strut and gobble awhile on a ridge top or hillside.

"Be patient and don't blow that turkey away with too much loud, fancy calling," says Hale. "Sit tight and soft-call. It might take an hour or longer, but if no hens show up, that gobbler will come to you."

Later in the morning, "cutting and running" in the hills is a good way to strike toms that lounge in the sun and strut for hens. Stay high, where you can see and hear well, "but don't walk along the tops of ridges," Hale explains. "Gobblers like to strut on high points and on long, open ridges where they can see well. To keep from spooking 'em, ease along the sides of ridges, where you have more cover. Hike along a trail or logging road if you can."

Pause every couple hundred yards and blow a crow call or cutt on a turkey call. Put some zing into those calls to shock gobbles from the mostly silent strutters. When a bird roars, go after him.

"If a bird gobbles on the side of a ridge or down in a hollow, try to circle around and approach him from the opposite side and above," points out Hale. "When you get close, slip up near the crest of the ridge and set up. If you're smart, you can sneak up on a lot of mountain turkeys that way."

By the way, don't forget to use your binoculars as you "run and gun." Anytime you can sneak up to a point and glass a gobbler in a draw, creek bottom or field below, you've got a huge tactical advantage. You can maneuver around and down and set up tight before calling to the bird. That ups your odds of reeling him in.

Here's one last tactic for attracting a mountain gobbler. Say you cutt on a box and a tom bellows across a draw and up on a ridge 250 yards away. Slip out to the edge of the hill you're on and call to him a couple more times. If he gobbles closer and seems to be working off the ridge and toward you, sit down and keep calling. Look and listen for him to cross the draw and strut up the near slope to you.

Ah, but nine out of ten times you won't be so lucky. A tom might roar at your yelps and cutts, but he'll stay planted on that ridge 200 to 250 yards away. Remember what we said earlier? You'll probably have to maneuver over to that same ridge to call him in.

Go to the bird, but not on a straight line. "I rarely make a beeline to a turkey, especially in hill country," says Hale. "Instead, I like to circle around, stay above a gobbler or at least on the same level with him, and feel my way along. I like to hear a turkey gobble a couple more times during my approach so I can get an idea exactly where he is. Sometimes I blow a crow call. If a turkey is fired up, he'll shock-gobble and give away his strut zone."

Sneak in tight and float a few soft calls. If you're lucky, you'll spot a crinkly white head bobbing up the slope any time now.

Field Turkeys

I knelt in the woods and watched the turkey in the pasture do his thing. When he strutted and drummed, his whole body shook. He turned on a dime, hoping hens in all directions would see him. A beard as thick as a whiskbroom poked from his chest. He was a magnificent if gaudy critter.

The turkey twirled away and his huge fan hid his eyes. I jogged ten steps, belly-flopped to the ground and crawled out to the edge of the field. I yelped. The tom whirled my way, dropped to half-strut and cut loose a stream of bombastic gobbles. We carried on like that for an hour. Finally the bird turned, deflated his strut as if I had poked him with a needle, waddled away and vanished into the far woods. Had I spooked him? Nah. That old devil was just being a "field turkey," darn unpredictable and tough to hunt.

Some gobblers roost on the edge of a crop field or pasture and sail out into

the middle of it to strut at first light. But most mornings you'll find turkeys roosted 100 yards or deeper in woods that rim a field. In this situation you can really outsmart yourself. You figure a tom will fly down and head for a nearby field to gather hens. So a good strategy would be to hang back, set up on the edge of the strut zone and whack him when he shows up, right? Well, wrong.

A gobbler has a knack for pitching down from his roost and taking a roundabout way through the woods to a strutting area. Most of the time he'll skirt your field-side calling and pop out into a field 80 to 100 yards away. He might as well be a mile away. Once a turkey bypasses your blind and heads out into the thin air to strut, it's tough—I dare say impossible—to call him back into shotgun range.

I believe it is best to sneak down the edge of a pasture in the pre-dawn gloom and go to a gobbler roosted back in the woods. Slip in tight and set up. That way you become a close

QUICK TIP

◆◆◆◆◆◆◆◆

"Wherever you hunt, study topo maps and scout a lot," says David Hale. "The more you know about the lay of the land, the easier it is to approach and move on gobblers. If you know how the ridges and drainages run in an area, and where logging roads and field edges are, you can move fast toward turkeys and set up to call in the best spots."

◆◆◆◆◆◆◆◆

and convenient "hen." Why should a bird pitch down and walk a couple hundred yards to a field when he can strut a little way and find you right away? It works–sometimes.

Hale points out another reason to hunt back in the woods early. "A lot of mornings two or three subordinate toms–I'm not talking about jakes, but two- or three-year-old turkeys with long beards– roost near an old boss gobbler," he says. "When the boss gobbles, the subordinates shut up. If the old turkey flies down and struts off for a field, the subordinates hang back in the woods. If you hang around in there with them, you might call in one of them."

Of course a lot of times it doesn't work out that way. Many mornings a turkey, be it a boss or a subordinate tom, will thump down from the roost, shun your yelps and take off gobbling toward a field. Well, don't just sit there, get up and go!

"Circle around and set up on the far edge of the field, in front of the turkey," says Hale. "Make it quick. Once the bird is heading in your direction, your calls might pull him over for a look. It doesn't always work out, but it's worth a shot."

Say you hunt in the timber one morning and get skunked. Around 9:00 a.m. you ought to set off and cover some country. Check for hens feeding and toms strutting in a nearby pasture (or in a food plot, burn, cutover or other open terrain). But don't mess up. One of the biggest mistakes hunters make is to walk smack down a logging road or trail that empties into a field. Sure, a gobbler might be blown up like a medicine ball out there, alone or with a harem of hens. But if you bumble out into plain view, he'll see you, deflate and run off in that body-rocking, beard-swinging gait that makes your heart sink.

"Sneak slowly through the woods and brush that rim a field," suggests Hale. "Use the lips of ridges, draws, high creek banks and other features of the terrain to cover your moves. Stop often, look through the trees and glass for turkeys out in the open."

If you don't spot a gobbler, try to raise one that might be strutting in a swale, behind a bend in a field or in a nearby fringe of woods. Blow a crow call or cutt on a box or aluminum pot. Really hit that call to make a turkey shock-gobble.

Let's say you spot a strutter or raise a gobble a couple hundred yards away. "Hang back in the woods–I can't make that point enough–and sneak or even crawl toward the bird," says Hale.

When you get close, look for a setup. A corner or point that juts out into a field is a great calling spot. See an old logging road or horse trail? If so, set up nearby. I've shot quite a few birds that strutted along two-tracks near fields. "Whenever you can set up on or near the highest spot in a field, or along an edge that leads to that high point, do it," Hale adds. "A field turkey might not go to that spot first thing in the morning, but he will end up there sometime during the day. It's a good place for him to strut and be seen by hens."

Sometimes you can set up, yelp and watch with awe as a gobbler waddles 200 yards across a field or plain, legs churning and beard swinging as he comes to you. When that happens, you know you hit the phase of the breeding season just right. The toms are hot and running to calls. But most of the time a field turkey is not so easy. Think about it. When you call from the edge of a field, burn, clear-cut or the like, a gobbler will hear your calls, but he will see no hen over there. That makes him leery of coming over.

You can troubleshoot that dilemma by using decoys (except if you hunt in Alabama, where fakes are prohibited). When a tom is out of sight, sneak or crawl out into a wide-open space and stake out a hen or two and maybe a jake. If a strutter hears your calls and sees your fakes, he may put two and two together and come on over for a look. Or he may spot your decoys, yawn and continue giving you a wide berth. I told you a field turkey is an unpredictable devil!

Hale sometimes sets up back in the woods, 20 yards or so off of a field. "Back in there, I don't fool with decoys," he says. "I just call like a hen hiding in the cover and playing hard to get. A gobbler might get curious, strut toward the edge of the field and boom, you can get him."

According to the Kentucky pro, one good thing about hunting a field turkey is that you can watch the bird's reaction to your calls. "A gobbler will tell you by his body language how much or how little to call," says Hale. "If a turkey blows up and struts toward your calls, keep them up. But if you call a lot and a turkey drops strut and walks a few yards away, tone down. Read a field turkey and give him what he likes."

As a rule, the more you call, the more an old tom will stand out in the grass and strut. "It's generally best just to let a field turkey know you're there," says Hale. "Give him some clucks, yelps and purrs and maybe the occasional excited cutt. Give a gobbler a lot of time to commit to the edge where you're set up."

Swamp Gobblers

The predawn was thick with humidity and mosquitoes. The moon shone pale and eerie on the stagnant pools of water. Cypress trees with dangling moss looked like the gates to a not-so-nice place. Wild things splashed and screeched. Then, *obblllle*, a turkey called deep in the Mississippi swamp.

"There," whispered Hale.

"Yeah, but how do we get to him?" I didn't relish the thought of wading into that snaky-looking place.

"There's a boat down by the slough," drawled Hale. "We'll hop over to him."

We piled into the canoe and paddled 100 yards to a strip of dry hardwoods. The gobbler bellowed again, but he was still a good 200 yards away, across another backwater.

"Let's sit right here," said Hale. "This is the biggest chunk of dry ground around. That bird might fly down and come to us. You never know."

I hate to set up a country mile from a turkey, especially on the opposite side of water, but in this case my friend's theory made sense. Besides, if we paddled or sloshed any closer, we might spook the turkey. We sat and called for 20 minutes, framing our clucks and yelps with cackles and cutts just as swamp hens do when flying and hopping across water.

The tom gobbled hard on the roost and clammed up at fly-down time. I knew he had either sailed deeper into the bog or was coming to us. *Garrrooobbbbleee,* he roared, 80 yards away! The bird hopped one last creek and strutted in, and I took him.

"This is what it's all about," said Hale as he smoothed the bird's jet-black feathers and checked out his sharp, curved hooks. "An old swamp turkey is about as wild and tough as they come."

Some mornings you have no choice but to suck it up and go to an Eastern or Osceola tom that gobbles deep in a swamp. Slip into a pair of burleys or hip boots, or get slick like Hale and I did and use a canoe or jon boat.

As you wade the muck and stagnant black water, be careful. I don't just mean looking out for snakes or gators. You need to be careful of your whereabouts—and the bird's. A swamp's thick air and moss-laden trees suck up a lot of noise and deaden a turkey's gobbling. A bird is usually roosted or strutting a lot closer than he sounds.

"A turkey can see a long way in a flat swamp, maybe 300 yards or farther," explains Hale. "You'll bump a lot of birds if you're not careful. Use vegetation and banks or humps for cover as you approach a gobbler. The humps may be only three to five feet high, but they'll help hide you."

Try to get close to a gobbler, but not too close. If you find a chunk of dry ground—an island, ridge, oak hammock or the like—within calling range of a tom, try setting up there. You might be 200 yards or so away from him, but that is okay. Call seductively and mix in hen cutts and cackles.

"I believe swamp gobblers roost over water for security," notes Hale, "but some mornings they sail a long way. A turkey might pitch across a slough and touch down on an island where he struts and gobbles for hens. That's where you need to be."

Move in, play it safe and call from the most convenient strip of dry ground in an area. You might tote a big tom out of the bog.

Sometimes you can shoot a swamp turkey without even getting your feet wet. Many Eastern and Osceola longbeards roost on the edges of swamps and head out into nearby pastures or crop fields at first light to gather hens. Ride back roads or hike around and glass for strutters on the edges of wetlands. If you find one, try to pattern him.

If a turkey sails out of a swamp near the same spot two or three days in a row, come back the next morning, set up on the edge and try to ambush him. In this case I wouldn't do a lot of loud, fancy calling. Just sit and listen for the bird to gobble deep in the swamp at dawn. Float a few yelps and clucks from your field-side setup. If you're lucky and have done your homework well, the tom might sail or strut out of the bog close by.

Let's say that one morning, a gobbler can't find any hens to breed on a water-rimmed island or ridge. He struts out of a swamp and into a pasture, but no girls are feeding there either. "Now an old turkey might start traveling," says Hale, "especially if it's late in the season. He might move from one swamp to the next, trying to gobble up hens. If you can find a dry strip of woods that connects two big swamps, that would be a good spot to set up and call in a swamp turkey."

No matter where you hunt, those toms are bound to be unpredictable. But knowing your way around the terrain and learning the habits of turkeys are the real keys to the game.

Like terrain, foliage plays a key role in how you hunt and call turkeys.

When foliage is thin in early spring:

• Hit your best spots 30 minutes earlier than normal each morning. Hope a gobbler roars early, and then sneak toward his roost under cover of darkness.

• Don't tear off after a turkey through sparse foliage, or you're apt to get busted. Instead, stay calm and scan the terrain. Without leaves and brush to cover your moves, you'll need to use the lip of a ridge, a draw, a creek bed or a similar wrinkle in the terrain to close the gap between you and the tom.

• Stop and glass frequently as you hunt. Turkeys can see a long way through thin woods, but then so can you. Anytime you spot a strutter on a ridge or a flock of hens towing a longbeard through a bottom, you obviously have a huge advantage.

• Play it safe. Conventional wisdom says to sneak within 100 yards or so of a tom before setting up to call. But before the brush and leaves blossom, that can be nearly impossible. Use terrain wrinkles to slip only as close as you dare to a roosted or strutting bird. You might have to set up 150 or even 200 yards away from him.

• Give a gobbler something to gawk at. Is it any wonder that he's reluctant to hang up in open woods? He hears your calls but doesn't see a hen over there. Okay, so put out a couple of hen decoys. Or, try to rile up an old turkey and pull him close by staking out a fake jake.

• Don't call too aggressively. In barren woods your yelps and cutts carry a long way. To keep a bird from pinning you down, cast soft calls out front and to the left and right. That helps to keep a tom drifting through open timber as he wonders where the heck that hen is.

When foliage pops out later in the spring:

• Listen closely. Remember that thick leaves muffle gobbles. It may sound as if a tom's roosted 400 yards away when he's perched on a limb at half that distance. You might think a strutter is way over on the next ridge when he's 100 yards up ahead on a flat or bench, gobbling every now and then. As you go to a turkey, stop a couple of times to listen and confirm a bird's location so you won't walk right over him.

• Leaves and ground foliage hide you well. On most mid-season and late-spring hunts, you should be able to slip within 125 or even 100 yards of a roosted or strutting turkey, and sometimes you can close the gap even more.

• In thick woods, a tom might be able to see only 30 to 40 yards in places, so he must strut close to check out your calls. That's good. But think about it. If a turkey can't see very far, neither can you. Every patch of timber has open holes, lanes and chutes here and there. Set up in and around these little brush breaks, where you can spot incoming toms. Remember this: It makes no sense to call a turkey to a spot so thick you can't see to shoot him!

• Leaves and brush soak up not only gobbles but also the sounds of your calls. Yelp and cutt a little louder than you did earlier in the season, especially when walking and trying to strike a bird. When a turkey gobbles, slip in tight and scale back to soft yelps, clucks and purrs to seal the deal.

Hunting Public Land

with Dave Streb

Say "public land," and most hunters cringe and bellow, "No way, too many people!" But face it, that's life today. As access to private farms and woodlands dwindles across America, more and more hunters are forced to head to state wildlife-management areas and national forests. And you know what? Many of these people are finding lots of gobblers and less hunting pressure than you think.

"Some public lands—especially here in the Northeast, where there is excellent hardwood habitat—are like turkey farms," says Streb. "There are plenty of gobblers around. Heck, I know of some state lands that are better than private areas I hunt. Sure, you have to deal with other hunters, but it's not all that difficult to find good spots."

Think Rural

If you hunt public ground within an hour's drive of Atlanta or Chicago, or even a smaller city like Birmingham, Alabama, you'll face big crowds during opening week of turkey season. But simply by thinking rural, you can cut down on a lot of the pressure.

A few years ago a friend of mine scanned an atlas and located a wildlife management area that rimmed a huge lake out in the middle of nowhere. He called and said, "Let's check it out. The fishing and hunting might be good. What have we got to lose?"

That's the right attitude. Four of us drove up in April and pitched a

The Expert: **Dave Streb** of Cuba, New York, has hunted wild turkeys for more than three decades. The man honed his skills the hard way. A good many of Streb's hunts have occurred on national forests and state wildlife-management lands in New York, Pennsylvania and Massachusetts. To this day Streb, one of the honchos at Quaker Boy Game Calls, relishes the challenge of hunting wary public-land toms.

HUNT SAFE!

Take heed of these warnings:

• Don't load your shotgun until you are out of your vehicle and in the woods. Double-check that your gun is unloaded before putting it back in your truck.

• Say you close to within 125 yards of a gobbler and hear yelping nearby. Is it a hen or a hunter? Most of the time you can tell—a person typically calls a lot more and a lot louder than a hen. But if you have the slightest doubt, back off.

• Sneaking into good calling range is okay, but never stalk or crawl toward a gobbler. You could be mistaken for a bird moving around.

• Buy a camouflage vest with a pullout blaze-orange flap. As you hike around and call, make sure the flap is visible. Ditto when you tote a tom back to your truck.

• Don't use a gobble call or fighting-purr calls on public land. You might call up another hunter!

• Don't set out decoys, especially a red-headed jake. Another hunter may stalk your decoys, thinking they are the real thing.

• Set up to call in an open area where you can see well in all directions. If another hunter walks close, whistle or speak. Don't yell and startle him or her.

• Before you disengage your shotgun's safety, know your target. Make sure it is a tom turkey with a long beard. Double-check your target before you shoot.

camp. The bass fishing might have been great, but we never got around to wetting a line. You see, we were up to our gills in hard-gobbling turkeys! In four days we heard 60 different birds and limited out on longbeards. And here's the kicker. We saw only four trucks parked there each morning, and we never bumped into another hunter in the woods.

Don't hold your breath waiting for me to give away our secret spot. (I'll tell you this much: It's between the Atlantic and Pacific coasts.) Go find a spot for yourself! For starters, go online at www.realtree.com. Go to "Hunting Trip" at the top and click on "State DNRs." Click on the state you plan to hunt, go to the fish and game department's home page, and investigate a wide range of public lands. Download and print maps, brochures, regulations and other hunt-planning data.

Try to zero in on a couple of tracts located 100 miles or more from cities. Then phone or e-mail a state or regional turkey biologist. Ask about hunting pressure. If pressure in the spring is light, ask more questions. Be sure to inquire about recent turkey harvests and hatches.

It's generally best to avoid small- to medium-size tracts (1,000 acres or less), even if their annual gobbler harvest is high. Such lands are sure to be popular; expect to see moderate to heavy hunting pressure, especially during opening week and on weekends. Rather, try to locate a larger, out-of-the-way area that yields a middle-of-the-road turkey harvest each spring. Chances are better that you'll find lots of elbowroom and a good number of gobblers, especially if the late-spring turkey hatches have been good for two or three years in a row.

Gobblers in Secluded Spots

Here's the key to planning a quality hunt on a public area: Locate at least five or six toms (the more the better!) in spots that receive the lightest hunting pressure.

"For starters, get a good topo map of an area and look for places where you can get off roads and away from people," says Streb. The New York pro begins looking for good spots to hunt turkeys during fall deer season. A couple of weeks before the spring opener, he drives and walks as much public ground as he can, scouting ridges, draws and clearcuts and listening for gobbling. "The more toms you can locate in different areas, the better off you'll be when the season opens," he says. "Other people will hunt some of those turkeys, but not all of them."

Streb monitors logging roads, trails and other major access routes in a public area. If he finds a road that has been closed to vehicles recently, he marks it on a topo map and checks it out. "If the habitat is good back in there, you'll find turkeys," he says. "Best of all, you won't see many people."

On the other hand, the forest service or a conservation department might open up a road and impact your strategy in a different way. For years one of Streb's best turkey spots was a wildlife-management area in New York. The main road that ran through the property was rough and impassable, so the place received light hunting pressure.

Then one year, state workers came in, fixed the road and even put in hiking and snowmobile trails. "Now the place is easy to get to," says Streb. "You can drive into the middle of the area, park and hike down the trails after turkeys. Needless to say, there's a lot more pressure now, so I don't hunt that place as much as I once did. You need to be aware of changes like that. Constantly look for remote areas to hunt."

Morning Tactics

Streb drives to a hunting spot early—extra early—each morning. "I want to park my truck, hike into the woods and be standing in a spot where I expect to hear a turkey gobble before another hunter drives up anywhere close," he says. The competition might see Streb's truck and drive on by. Even if some guy parks and hikes in, "hopefully I will have had a good hunt and maybe even shot a gobbler before he gets back in there," says Streb.

Your best bet is to get your gobbler during opening week. (If you can hunt Monday through Friday, when fewer hunters are in the woods, great!) After that, things get iffy.

As the season progresses, most turkeys that open their beaks and gobble on the roost are apt to receive at least a light dose (if not a full barrage) of calling from other hunters. People tromp through the woods and spook hens and toms almost every day. The birds get skittish, and to trick 'em, you'd better get creative.

Let's say one evening you roost a gobbler on an oak ridge. Well, go home or back to camp and study a topo map or an aerial photograph. Chart a fresh course to the bird that will carry you off a well-used logging road or trail and up the backside of the ridge, around and through a thick bottom, across a creek…you get the idea. The next morning, go to that turkey from a direction other hunters would never dream of taking.

The sky's the limit when varying your approaches. I've used bass boats and canoes to get to gobblers that roost and strut in remote spots along lakes and rivers. I have a friend who pedals his mountain bike up and down ridges on a state area. Another guy I know rides his horse deep into a national forest. After tying up his mount, he climbs ridges, slips through creek drainages and approaches gobblers from offbeat angles.

Set up in fresh spots, but forget about the fancy yelping and cutting that are in vogue today. The calls might sound nice and cause a tom to gobble his head off, but that is the last thing you want. On a public area, the more a turkey gobbles, the more likely he is to call up another hunter. That can cause an unsafe situation, or at the very least, it can ruin your hunt. Besides, a wired gobbler generally responds best to soft, seductive calling. Use a mix of clucks, yelps and purrs to entice a tom off the roost and into gun range.

Midday Strategies

One April morning Streb and a buddy drove to one of their favorite spots in a Pennsylvania national forest. Six trucks were already parked there! The hunters motored off to another place they had scouted earlier. "Things

SALVAGE A HUNT

Hunt long enough on public land and something like this will happen: You're set up on a tom that is roaring at your calls and working in. Then you hear a box call or a diaphragm—another hunter has heard the turkey and is moving in too! The guy keeps coming; your turkey either sees him or doesn't like that calling, so he shuts up.

You naturally want to throw down your cap, cuss and run off to find another turkey to hunt. Not so fast. Sit quietly awhile (don't call again) and see what happens. For one thing, that is the safe thing to do. The less you move around and call when another hunter is close, the less chance of a potential conflict.

The hunter, incredulous as to why the turkey quit gobbling, should eventually leave. On the off chance he doesn't and walks closer, whistle or speak out to let him know you're there. But most of the time the other hunter will go, and good riddance. Now you might be able to salvage the hunt.

Wait another 15 to 30 minutes for the woods to settle down. Then float a yelp or an excited cutt. Chances are the turkey did not go far. If he's hot, he might start gobbling again, and this time he might come on in.

worked out fine," recalls the New York pro. "We called in a big gobbler and my friend got him."

About 9:30 a.m. Streb said to his pal, "Let's go back to that first spot, just for the heck of it." They did, and the other trucks and hunters were gone. Streb called and a gobbler roared! They worked that turkey the rest of the morning and left him gobbling at the noon quitting hour.

"I don't know, maybe one of those guys spooked the turkey off the roost early and shut him up for a while," says Streb. "All I know is that we were able to go back in there and have a great hunt. We didn't kill the turkey, but I went back and got him a few days later. Come to think of it, I shot him about 10:00 a.m."

You can have fun like that by hunting a state or federal area late in the morning or even in the afternoon (where legal). It's one of the best tactics going, and two things work to your advantage. One, most of your competition has left for home, work or camp, so the woods and the turkeys have settled back down. Two, by midmorning many hens have deserted the toms to lay eggs and sit on their nests. Cover lots of ground and blow a crow call or cutt on a turkey call—a tom or two is apt to roar.

Ah, but just because a turkey gobbles at your calls doesn't mean he'll come a-running. This is especially true if you set up near a road or trail where other hunters walked and called earlier in the day. Again, vary your approaches to a tom and set up in a fresh spot. Switch to soft clucks, yelps and purrs to close the sale and get him.

Late Spring: Prime Time

Perhaps the best time to hunt a public area is in late April or mid- to late May. "As the season winds down, the crowds subside with each passing day," notes Streb. "The last week you might not see another hunter."

By then, many hens have gone to nest. Still looking for love, some longbeards go into a gobbling frenzy, trying to hook up with the last receptive gals.

"Late in the season turkeys sometimes gobble as well or better than they did during opening week," notes Streb. "Some people say that public-land gobblers are call-shy, but not in this scenario. If you hit it right, you can yelp and cutt all you want and a big tom will run to your calls."

Putting Bachelors to Bed

with Mark Drury

The wind dies, the sun sinks and the whippoorwills begin their nighttime serenade. A hunter hikes out a misty ridge and owlhoots, *whoooooaaaa*. He calls again and hears, *garrroooobblle*. "All right!" the hunter whispers triumphantly, turning for the truck. "I'll be back to get that turkey in the morning."

"That roosting scenario is pretty typical, but other than knowing a gobbler is in the area, it really doesn't tell you much," says Mark Drury. The Missouri pro used to roost turkeys like most hunters do, but no more. These days he practically climbs into bed with the toms he locates on spring evenings. He roosts aggressively regardless of the turkey subspecies he is hunting.

"How many mornings has this happened to you?" Drury asks. "A turkey gobbles at first light. You sneak toward him. The sky brightens fast. You are forced to stop and sit down against a tree, knowing that if you move any closer the bird will probably see you and spook. But you know full well that you should set up 30 to 50 yards closer to the gobbler. Well, aggressive roosting the night before can put you up there where you need to be to kill a turkey."

The expert: **Mark Drury** of St. Peters, Missouri, has vision. When he founded M.A.D. Calls back in the mid-1990s, he didn't want to be just another turkey-call maker. The man had a mission: to build calls that would carry turkey calling to a higher level. Well, he succeeded. Drury's line of "high-frequency" mouth and friction calls make turkeys gobble like mad. Drury is also an innovator in the woods. He hunts and calls with a not-so-quiet confidence and aggressiveness, especially when putting toms to bed on spring evenings.

The Bedtime Ritual

Roosting is key to Drury's success, and he begins an hour or so before sunset each evening. He covers lots of country by truck, foot or, in some watery habitats, boat. He owl-hoots, crow-calls or cutts on a turkey call in hopes of striking a gobbler still on the ground and moving toward his roosting area.

"I try to make turkeys gobble and get on 'em in late afternoon, but the best time to locate birds is just when the wind lays and the sun disappears," he says. "By then, a turkey is on the limb, and tends to gobble better than he does on the ground."

When a tom bellows anywhere close, Drury drops everything and goes straight to him. "Roosting is a fun sport in itself," he says. "You're fighting the clock those last 5 to 10 minutes of good light, trying to get within 100 yards of a bird with the sun setting fast. Once it gets too dark, Eastern or Osceola turkeys won't gobble anymore. Merriam's and Rio Grande birds are different. Sometimes they'll gobble after dark."

Having slipped within the century mark of a roosted turkey, most hunters would feel pretty confident about the next morning's hunt. Not Drury, who tries to close that distance to 60 yards or so. "I wear camouflage and move slowly and carefully, using terrain and brush for cover," he says. "I look and listen for other turkeys flying up. While I'm taking those last few steps, I try to make the bird gobble one or two more times so I can hone in on his tree. I listen closely for drumming. In the end, I like to get where I can almost see the turkey."

Sometimes he can do just that. With binoculars, Drury scans the skyline for a strutter on a limb. "Once in a while you can catch the flash of a turkey's neck moving as he gobbles one last time," he says.

In tight with a tom, Drury studies the lay of the land. He looks for open spots and chutes where the bird might fly down and walk in to calling the next morning. Is there a gully, creek or similar hazard that might hang up the gobbler once he hits the ground? If so, Drury knows to take that out of play the next day. Finally, he looks for the best set-up tree. He then waits 15 minutes, until it's pitch black, before he sneaks out of the woods.

"At this point two things are critical," Drury says. "Always count the exact number of steps to a landmark 100 yards back in the direction of your truck–a fence corner, jump-off point in a logging road, whatever. And time precisely how long it takes to walk out of the woods and back to your vehicle."

Morning-After Strategies

For a tight roost to pay off, get up extra early the next morning. "You need to be in the woods and set up an hour earlier than normal," Drury says. "If you're late you can't get in there close without the turkey seeing you."

Park your vehicle and hike to the landmark you pinpointed the evening before. Sneak quietly toward the gobbler, retracing and counting the exact number of steps back in. Sit down against a tree, pull out your calls, prop your shotgun comfortably over your knees and get ready. After that, freeze.

"When the sky starts brightening, you can't afford to fiddle around for calls or move your gun, because the bird might see or hear you," Drury notes.

Now for the best part. Sit back and enjoy the ride. "Usually a turkey will start drumming in the dark an hour before he gobbles," says Drury. "That's awesome to hear. And the first time he gobbles, it's so loud and clear that you'll probably jump."

When the glow of the sun lathers the horizon, you might even look up and see the turkey on his limb 60 to 80 yards away. If so, study him. Watch the bird strut and run out his neck to gobble. When he quits gobbling, starts fidgeting around, looks at the ground and flexes his wings a couple of times, get ready–fly-down time is near! You might also see hens preening on limbs or "tree hopping" to get closer to the gobbler before pitching down. Watching all this action is fun, and it helps you immensely. You can see how gobblers and hens behave at first light, and that knowledge will come in handy when you set up and call on subsequent hunts.

Slipping close to a gobbler one morning, you might spook a nearby hen or two from their limbs. That's good! You'll have less calling competition from the real thing at sunrise. "Even if hens flush, chances are the gobbler won't bust out," Drury says. "If the turkey didn't see you in the darkness, he doesn't know why those hens spooked. Hens move around from tree to tree a lot. So keep on counting your steps and sneaking close to a gobbler."

HOW CLOSE IS TOO CLOSE?

A tight setup invites this question: Just how close might a gobbler pitch down in front of you at daybreak?

One morning in Nebraska, Drury and I slipped in on a tom we had roosted the evening before. An hour before sunrise the turkey boomed spit-and-drums. He gobbled and we flinched. With the sun peeking up in the east, Drury eked out a tiny tree call. The turkey crashed from his tree, and with his enormous wingspan, he looked like a prehistoric pterosaur flying in! I shot when the big bird's feet hit the ground 15 yards away.

But there's a flip side. You're going to bust a few turkeys when you roost aggressively and go for super-tight setups. "But I think you'll more than make up for that with the number of birds you get close to and take," Drury says. "The more you try the tactic, the fewer turkeys you'll spook. You'll learn to use terrain and foliage to cover your moves."

QUICK TIP

◆◆◆◆◆◆◆◆

Whichever locator call you use, don't keep pounding away on it as you sneak close to a roosted tom. Turkeys – Easterns and Osceolas in particular – don't gobble as much in the evenings as they do in the mornings. If you try to force things with too many hoots or coyote calls, you might spook them.

◆◆◆◆◆◆◆◆

Calling Tactics

If you call too much and too loudly to a tom roosted less than 100 yards away, you can blow him off the limb. At sunrise he might get nervous, pitch out the opposite side of the tree and glide several hundred yards away. Take it easy, and tailor your calls to a gobbler's position on a limb.

Normally a turkey flies down the way he's facing. If you can see a bird or, more likely, determine by his loud, clear-throated gobbling that he's facing you on the limb, it's probably best not to call. If you do call while a turkey is still in a tree, make it a barely audible cluck or yelp.

Anytime a tom is facing away from your setup, his gobbles floating out the far side of a tree, get a little bolder. "Tree-call to focus the bird's attention back your way," Drury says. "And use non-vocal turkey sounds. Slap your leg to sound like a hen pitching out, and then scratch some leaves on the ground. Toms will often gobble at and fly down to those sounds."

Final Thoughts

Drury says, "Aggressive roosting is one of my most consistently successful tactics. But I don't want to give the impression that it works all the time. I'd say that if you go out roosting ten evenings in a row, you'll get the tight setup we're talking about maybe once or twice."

Several factors have to come together for the strategy to work. A tom has to gobble frequently at your locator calls at sunset. He's got to roost in a spot where you can get to him quickly. There must be terrain and foliage for cover so you can sneak up that close to the bird.

When things pan out and you set up tight on a tom you roosted the night before, your chances of scoring a beard and spurs are high. "But even if you don't shoot a bird, it's still an awesome morning," says Drury. "In there close, you'll hear all sorts of turkey sounds, and you never know what you might see. That's fun and exciting."

MARK DRURY'S LOCATOR CLINIC

Here are five good pieces of advice:

• To roost Eastern turkeys, Drury mostly owl-hoots. "I hoot just once or twice in a spot before moving on. If a bird is roosted close, he'll usually gobble at my first hoots. If not, I'm gone, looking for a gobbler that will respond."

• The Missouri call maker starts out with a single barred owl hoot—*hooooahh.* "If a turkey is ready to rock, he'll answer that. And a one-note hoot won't block out a bird's gobble. If a turkey responds in the middle of a fancy eight-note hoot, you might not hear him. Keep it short and sweet."

• A coyote howler works best for locating Rio Grande and Merriam's turkeys out West. "Still, once in a while I howl or yip when roosting Easterns," adds Drury. "The good thing about a

coyote call is that it is loud and high-pitched, and you can get a lot of faraway turkeys to gobble at it. Even if you can't slip in tight to roost them, getting a general line on a long-range bird or two is important. If you don't shoot a turkey early one morning, you might have to go looking for a distant bird."

• Drury sometimes gets down on a crow call to sound like two black bandits fighting. "A lot of times I put raspy, gargling sounds in my crow calls in hopes of yanking a gobble out of a turkey."

• When creeping close to a tom that won't gobble much in the evening, Drury tries a quick cutt or cackle on a turkey call as a last resort. "Sometimes a turkey will gobble one time at a hen call and give away his roost tree."

CALLING
LONGBEARDS

Mastering Turkey Calls

with Will Primos

There are two basic kinds of calls: air-activated (mouth) and friction. A hunter may prefer one over the other depending on the situation.

Mouth calls have been around a long time. The first one was sold back in 1867 by Samuel MacLean, who called it the "bird and whistle call." In 1920, a man named Henry Bridges advertised a mouth call in *Field & Stream* magazine. These early air-activated calls were crude and large compared to those on the market today.

One kind of friction call, the pot-and-peg, has been around since the late 1880s, when the varieties were crafted of wood or even turtle shells, with crude slate surfaces fitted into them.

An Arkansan named Gibson patented the first hinged-lid box call back in 1897. Most are crafted of wood—maple, cherry, walnut or poplar—and have free-swinging wooden handles, or "lids." Simply scrape a lid across one side of a box to yelp.

Another friction call you ought to try is the push-pin (some hunters call it the push-peg or the push-button). It is a small, wooden or plastic box with a spring-loaded pin running through it. Attached to the pin is a wooden, slate or glass plate. When you work the pin, it strikes a surface inside the box.

The Expert: In 1976 **Will Primos** of Jackson, Mississippi, began tinkering with turkey calls. Working in his garage at night and on weekends, he cut frames from tin beer cans and fitted them with rubber reeds. Turkey hunters across the South, and then across the United States, began gobbling up his mouth calls, and the rest is history. Primos now owns a state-of-the-art call-making facility, and he and his staff crank out some of the best diaphragm and friction calls on the market. Here the call maker offers invaluable tips and techniques for mastering the various devices.

The Diaphragm Call

The most common air-activated call is the diaphragm call. It features one or more latex or prophylactic reeds crimped into an aluminum frame. A tape skirt covers the frame and acts as an air seal. The best diaphragms are hand-stretched and hand-tuned.

Some models of diaphragm calls have one or two rubber reeds; others have three or four reeds. Many calls have clipped or notched reeds, which "tend to put a lot of rasp into your yelps," notes Primos.

One highly touted advantage of the diaphragm is its hands-free operation. "You can sit, call and hold your shotgun or bow, and move it easily when you need to," says Primos. Since the diaphragm is obviously not affected by moisture (saliva on the reeds actually enhances the sound), the call is the best choice for a rainy day.

How to Use It

Place a diaphragm in your mouth with the open reeds facing forward. Tongue the call up into the roof of your mouth. It shouldn't sit too far forward or too far back. Your tongue should touch all the reeds and extend about a half-inch beyond the front of the call.

If a call feels too wide and bulky, you can trim the tape skirt a little. "Trim the sides of the call first, and then the back," advises Primos. "Trim a little at a time until the call feels just right. You can also slightly bend down the

aluminum frame to make the call fit comfortably and create a better air seal in the roof of your mouth."

According to the Mississippi call maker, there are two major keys to using the diaphragm. "First, don't just blow air across the reeds, but bring it up from deep in your diaphragm. And work your jaw up and down when you call, just like when you talk."

Primos points out that everybody calls a little differently. He shows lots of jaw movement when he runs a diaphragm, but you might move your jaw less. "Still, you've got to move your jaw up and down to some degree to talk turkey, and especially to make two-note yelps," he says.

Now, on to mocking the major hen vocalizations on a mouth call:

• To cluck like a turkey on the roost or on the ground, "pop air across the reeds while saying the word 'puck' or 'putt,'" says Primos. While you might drop your jaw a little bit, clucking is more about popping or smacking your lips.

• To cutt like a hen in the spring, string together a series of sharp, fast and irregular clucks. "Cutts have a staccato quality, with notes that go up and down," says Primos. Vary the amount of air you force across a call's reeds while popping your lips.

• To mock the two-note yelp of a hen—the bread-and-butter call you'll use most in either spring or fall—"you need to slur a high note and a low note together," suggests Primos. "Say the

QUICK TIP

❖❖❖❖❖❖❖❖

Say you use a single-frame diaphragm call with two or more reeds. When those reeds are dry, they stick together. "Some people try to pull the reeds apart or keep them separated with toothpicks, but I don't worry about it," says Will Primos. "I just pop a call into my mouth, roll it around and get it good and wet with saliva before I call to a turkey. The reeds loosen up pretty quickly and roll into a call that sounds just fine."

❖❖❖❖❖❖❖❖

Two types of diaphragm calls: Primos' Diamond Yelper (left) has a notched reed for a distinctive, raspy sound. The True Double (right), with a 1/16-inch separation between the reeds, is easy for many callers to use and control.

word 'chalk' while moving your jaw up and down." Practice a lot to get the speed and cadence of your yelps just right.

• To cackle like a hen flying down from the roost at daybreak, string together some fast, excited yelps. Primos recommends saying "kit-kit-kit-kit-kat-kat-kat-kow-kow-kow" while running air rapidly across a call's reeds.

• To kee-kee or whistle like a young turkey in the fall, say "pee-pee-pee." Pin a call tightly to the roof of your mouth to create a good air seal. Then bring your lips tightly together and let the whistles come out. To roll into the kee-kee run, a call young gobblers often make in the fall, back up your "pee-pee-pee" with a couple of "chalk-chalk" yelps.

• To purr like a feeding or contented hen, pin a call to the roof of your mouth, push air up from your chest and flutter the back of your throat. "Another way to purr is to flutter the back of your tongue," notes Primos. Sound tough? Well, it is, and some hunters have a devil of a time purring on a mouth call. Keep practicing until you get it, or try purring on a pot-and-peg call instead.

The Pot-and-Peg Call

Today pot-and-peg calls are more popular than ever. You can use a finely machined wooden, plastic or graphite cup into which is glued a slate, glass, ceramic, aluminum or copper surface. To talk turkey, strike a surface with a peg made of hickory, ash, rosewood, acrylic or carbon. "This type of turkey call is probably the easiest to use," says Primos, "and man, it sounds great."

A pot-and-peg call is remarkably versatile. You can use just a little hand pressure on a call to cluck and purr softly; that's deadly for closing the sale with a longbeard. Or you can bear down on a striker and make the woods ring with loud, high-pitched yelps or cuts to shock a gobble from a tom a half-mile away.

If you don't carry at least three pots (with different surfaces) and a variety of pegs in your vest, you're messing up big-time. "All of the surfaces and pegs give you different sounds," says Primos. "By switching from a slate to a glass to an aluminum call, and using a wooden or a carbon peg on each of those surfaces, you can make all sorts of high-pitched or raspy calls. That variety is what you want."

How to Use It

The biggest mistake people make is to grip both pot and peg with white knuckles. Man, lighten up!

MAKE IT A DOUBLE

When I traveled to Mississippi in the mid-1980s to hunt with Will Primos for the first time, I must admit I was pretty lousy on a diaphragm call. The call maker stuck one of his True Doubles in my face and said, "Try this."

The call was twice as thick as the other diaphragms I'd tried, and it took some getting used to. Then I went out and yelped a few times and fooled a big old Mississippi gobbler. I've been a fan of stacked-frame calls ever since.

A Primos True Double has a pair of aluminum frames stacked and glued, one on top of the other. The fat call feels weird at first, but after awhile you'll notice how snugly it fits into the roof of your mouth. Since a double-frame doesn't float around in your mouth like a single call sometimes does, it is easy to control and seal air with minimal tongue pressure.

"To yelp on the call, huff air up from your chest while moving your jaw up and down, just as you would when using a single-frame diaphragm," says Primos. "The two-note yelps you produce will have a distinctive raspy tone."

At first you might think a stacked-frame call has too much rasp. Well, you might not win a calling contest with a True Double, but its heavy rasp will fool a bunch of toms in the woods. In addition to clucking, yelping and cutting like a gravel-voiced hen, I like to "yawk" slowly and coarsely on a double-frame. The call is great for mimicking gobbler clucks and yelps in spring or fall.

By design, the rubber reeds of a stacked-frame call are staggered and spaced about 1/16-inch apart. Every time you use the call, whether it is dry or wet with saliva, it rolls nicely into two-note yelps. The first yelp you give a gobbler is always right on the money, and that gives you confidence.

A stacked-frame call costs a little more than a single-reed diaphragm, but it's worth it. Keep the call clean and store it in a cool place, and it will last a long time.

The bottom line: If you're having trouble talking turkey on a single-frame diaphragm, or if you just want to experiment with something different, give a stacked-frame call a whirl.

On a rainy or misty morning, strike a glass or aluminum pot with a carbon peg. No matter how wet the call's surface gets, the carbon peg will still grab it and create friction. You can yelp or cutt without missing a beat.

◆◆◆

A box call often clucks and yelps on its own as you hike around the woods. To quiet the call, place a folded napkin or a piece of cloth (a spare camo facemask works great) between the handle and sounding lips, and then wrap a stout rubber band around the call. Some chalk will rub off on the napkin or cloth, so be sure to chalk the call again before using it.

◆◆◆◆◆◆◆◆

Pot-and-peg calls are made from various materials: slate, glass, aluminum, etc. This model can be strapped to your leg or gun for one-handed operation.

If you're right-handed, hold a pot lightly between the fingertips of your left hand. (Do the reverse if you're left-handed.) Grasp a peg as if you were writing with a pencil. Hold the call out in front of your body to keep from muting the sounds.

"You'll produce the best sound if you stabilize and control the call," explains Primos. A good way to do that is to brace your "peg hand" against the side of the pot and then work the striker. Be sure to keep your fingers off a call's surface and the tip of a peg. The natural oils from your skin will moisten the surfaces and affect the sound of your calls.

Hold a striker at about a 45-degree angle to a call's surface, and then run it lightly. "It's all in that 'angle of attack,'" notes Primos. Tweak the way you hold a peg to make the various calls.

Here's something to remember: Work a peg in the middle of a call's surface to make deep clucks and yelps. Move the striker out to the edge of a call for more trilling notes.

To create friction and make a call ring true, rub its surface frequently with an abrasive pad or sandpaper. And don't forget to roughen the tip of a wooden striker from time to time.

Now, on to making the key calls:

• To cluck, place a peg on a pot, angle it slightly inward and pull a short stroke. Do not pick the peg up off the surface–let it skip across the slate or glass. Put just a little pressure on the peg to cluck softly. Bear down harder on the striker for louder and more animated clucks.

• To cutt, serve up a series of fast, broken clucks. Bear down fairly hard on a peg and skip it over a call's surface for five seconds or more, but again, don't pick up the peg. Remember, there is no rhythm or cadence to cutting.

• To yelp, run a peg on a surface in straight lines or ovals. Primos prefers the oval attack. "I make small ovals for soft yelps. I put a little more pressure on the peg and expand the size of the ovals for louder yelps."

• To cackle, string together a few fast, raspy yelps. "I often finish up with a few reassuring clucks, like a hen often makes once she flies down from the roost and hits the ground," says the Mississippi calling guru.

• To purr, exert just enough pressure on a peg so that it skips lightly over a call's surface. Run little straight lines or make half-circles. Purring on a slate call is tough to beat for pulling a tom those last few yards into gun or bow range.

The Box Call

This friction call is a snap to use. Pick one up, fiddle with it for a few minutes, and you'll be talking dang good turkey. A finely tuned box makes, arguably, the most realistic yelp of any of the turkey calls. Moreover, the box is great for cutting loudly to locate toms late in the morning or in the afternoon.

A box is big and bulky to carry, but your hunting vest probably has a long box-call pocket, so the size is no big deal. Running a box does require some hand movement, but again, no biggie. It's easy to hide a box in your lap or behind your knees as you work a turkey. When a bird struts in close, simply drop the box into your lap and take him.

How to Use It

Many people hold a box with a vise grip. Big mistake! Finesse the call to make sweet turkey sounds. Hold a box lightly in your left palm and work the lid gently with the fingers of your right hand (vice versa for lefties). "Be sure to keep your fingers off the sides of a box so you won't deaden its sound," Primos cautions.

Some people run a box best with a

vertical hold. Lay a call in the palm of your hand, turn your hand perpendicular to the ground and scrape the lid up and down.

Chalk a box call before you hit the woods and a couple of times during a hunt. "Use only wax-free chalk," notes Primos. "It creates the best friction and it won't gum up the grain of the wood."

Now, for the calls:

• To cluck on a box, simply pop the handle lightly on the call's sounding lip. "Another way to do it is to hold the call in your palm, press your thumb lightly on the top of the lid and tap it with your other hand," says Primos. "That's how I do it."

• To cutt, bear down on the handle a little bit and pop or tap a series of fast, sharp clucks. The vertical hold works great for cutting.

• To yelp, move the handle an inch or less off to the side of the sounding lip and "close the box" to run two notes together. "Light pressure on the lid will give you raspy yelps," notes Primos. "Put a little more pressure on the handle for higher-pitched notes."

• To purr, set the lid off to the side of the sounding lip and drag it softly across the lip of the box.

Here are several good manufacturers of turkey calls:

Knight & Hale
P.O. Drawer 670
5732 Canton Road
Cadiz, KY 42211
1-800-500-9357
270-924-1755
www.knight-hale.com

Quaker Boy, Inc.
5455 Webster Road
Orchard Park, NY 14127
1-800-544-1600
716-662-3979
www.quakerboygame calls.com

Primos Hunting Calls
604 First Street
Flora, MS 39071
1-800-622-8076
www.primos.com

M.A.D. Calls
Lohman Calls
4500 Doniphan Drive
Neosho, MO 64850
1-800-922-9034
417-451-4438
www.outland-sports.com

Hunter's Specialties
6000 Huntington Court NE
Cedar Rapids, IA 52402
319-395-0321
www.hunterspec.com

Box calls come in many sizes and styles, each with a unique volume and tone. A box call shines for mimicking raspy hen yelps, and for cutting to locate or "strike" toms.

TUBE & WINGBONE CALLS

A mouth diaphragm gives you either trilling or deep-pitched notes. Most friction calls have lots of rasp. To round out your calling arsenal, carry a tube (right) and a wing-bone (below) in your vest. A tube call consists of a small tube fitted with a latex reed. It is great for producing hollow-sounding clucks and yelps. You can also gobble or mock the "aggravated purr" of two gobblers fighting.

The key to running a tube is to fit your lower lip properly on the call's reed. This takes a lot of practice, as each call company makes its tubes a little differently.

Tipping a tube slightly upward might help you position your lips just right for clucks and two-note yelps. Don't blow into the call, but huff air up from your chest as if you were calling on a diaphragm.

The wingbone is one of the oldest and most unique turkey calls, a staple with Native Americans and old-timers in the South. A traditional wing-bone uses the small radius bone from a turkey's wing as the mouthpiece; a larger bone or a hollow cow horn serves as the sounding bell. Today, Primos and a couple of other call companies offer replica wingbones made of plastic and other modern materials.

With a wingbone you are pretty much limited to clucks and yelps. To make them, huff air up from your chest while kissing or smacking your lips into the call's mouthpiece. The melodious, trilling calls float a long way through the woods. A gobbler might roar back in the spring, or cluck or yelp in response in autumn.

The Push-Pin Call

By design, the push-pin call is not very loud, so it works best for soft, seductive clucks, yelps and purrs. It is easy to use, and it's a great choice for beginners and kids. But veterans like Primos use it too. "It gives me another sound in my calling routine," he says.

How to Use It

Hold the call lightly in one hand and simply press the top of the pin with your forefinger to yelp. For louder yelps, pull longer strokes on the bottom of the pin. To cluck, tap the pin against the palm of your hand or your leg. Speed up those clucks to cutt.

This push-pin call is a gun-mountable design with an elastic strap for minimum hand movement.

The Fine Art of Working a Gobbler

with Eddie Salter

One fine spring morning, a tom rips double and triple gobbles on a ridge. You sneak toward the bird, flop down beside a big oak tree, pull out your calls and begin yelping and cutting like mad. The tom roars back and takes a couple of steps your way. Man, you're working that turkey now!

Or are you?

Actually you're not, because there is a big—no, make that huge—difference between calling to a gobbler and working him. The caller runs to a turkey and tosses out a mother lode of clucks, yelps, cackles and cuts. Maybe a few of those calls stick, and the bird comes a-running. But I wouldn't bet your 401k on it.

On the other hand, the working hunter has a plan. He or she sneaks toward a gobbler and sets into motion a well-conceived and multi-dimensional strategy, like the one Eddie Salter lays out here. Try it and take this to the bank—you'll trick your share of longbeards.

The Expert: **Eddie Salter** of Evergreen, Alabama, called in and shot his first gobbler when he was 10 years old. The boy got hooked, and he has made turkey hunting his passion and his career. Salter, who has won many state and national turkey-calling titles over the years, is a pro-staff member for H.S. Strut game calls and one of the most sought-after seminar speakers in the outdoor industry. At nearly every one of his talks a hunter will stand up and ask, "Man, just how do you work a gobbler?" Well, here's how.

The Setup

You can be the best caller in the world, but you won't fool gobblers on a regular basis if you sit and yelp in poor locations. "The setup lays the foundation for working a turkey, no doubt about it," says Salter. "As you move in on a gobbling bird, and before you ever call to him, look for a good place to set up. Try to pick a tree in a fairly flat area where you can see and shoot 40 yards out front and also to the left and right."

Avoid overly thick ridges or bottoms—circle around and set up where a gobbler can strut to you through an open lane or chute in the woods. You might already know this, but Salter says it bears repeating: "Take anything that might hang up a turkey, like a creek, fence or deep gully, out of play." Your goal is to make it easy and convenient for a gobbler to work to your calls.

Whenever possible, select a tree that sits slightly above an open flat, bench or bottom where you think a strutter might show up. An extra foot or two of elevation increases your visibility as you scan the woods.

After setting up, don't start hammering a bird with yelps, cackles and cutts. "Chill out, sit back for a minute and listen to the sounds of the woods," suggests Salter.

Read a Turkey

Some birds bellow long and hard, while others gobble more sporadically. Some toms move around and brazenly search for hens. Others are more skittish and aloof, strutting in one spot and waiting for girls to come to them. In a word, all turkeys are individuals. That is why you should read each bird and tailor your calls accordingly.

"I like to set up and start a turkey with what I call a little 'running cutt' on a mouth call, and I back that up with a couple of fairly aggressive yelps," says Salter. "Then I listen and read the bird. If he gobbles right back and cuts me off, I feel like I can get pretty aggressive with him. But if he doesn't gobble at that first call, or if he hesitates before gobbling, I generally back off. I call less aggressively to a turkey like that. And sometimes I switch over to soft stuff on a slate call."

Switching calls can be vitally important in the initial stages of working a turkey. One April morning I set up on a roosted tom and hit him with some tree clucking and yelping on a stack-frame diaphragm. Man, it sounded pretty, if I may say so myself. I perked up my ears and listened. The bird not only failed to gobble back, he shut up! Was this one of those knuckleheads that had no intention of working? Maybe, but I rolled right into Plan B, changing over to a high-pitched aluminum call with a hickory striker. I clucked and yelped. The turkey bellowed and flew down my way! I worked the bird with tinny clucks and yelps, and shot him at 17 steps. "It all has to do with that individualistic thing," notes Salter. "One morning a turkey might shun your favorite mouth call, and you'll think, 'This bird ain't gonna work.' But change to a slate or box call, and that turkey might roar and blow the cap off your head."

You need to remember that on any given day, a turkey might like the tone and pitch of one calling device over all others. Don't be afraid to try a variety of air and friction calls. Once you get a bird fired up and gobbling at one call, he's ready to work.

Close the Sale

You're set up and calling, and a bird is gobbling and coming. Now you're working! Continue to read the frequency and intensity of a tom's calls. As a general rule, the more and harder a turkey gobbles, the more fancy yelping and cutting you can get away with. However, if a bird gobbles lightly and sporadically, tone it down. He might be an old, pressured bird, or simply one of those aloof three-year-olds that takes his sweet time working to a call. But nothing is set in stone. Again, each turkey and each hunting situation is different. Go with your gut feeling as to how much and how aggressively to call.

"You should remember one thing, though," notes Salter. "The more you call, the more often a turkey stops, stands out there and gobbles. And the more he gobbles, the greater the chance that he'll call up a hen."

If a bird is thundering and coming on a string, or if he's closing fairly fast, back off the calling a bit. This keeps a turkey drifting your way and increases your chances of killing him quickly, before he gobbles up a hen, shuts up and leaves you holding the bag.

Many toms will seem to be working nicely to your calls, gobbling and closing the gap from 120 yards to 100 to 80...but just when you think you've got him, he pulls the dreaded hang-up 60 to 75 yards out. Should you call again, or be quiet and be patient? It's a dilemma you'll face many times during a spring season.

"If you suspect you're working an old turkey that has been fooled with and maybe even shot at by another hunter, tone down or shut up and give

MOVING SHOP

No matter how deftly you set up and call, there's a chance you'll have to move to fool a gobbler. "If a turkey is hot, he should come in 15 minutes or so," notes Eddie Salter. "Sometimes I sit and call for 30 minutes. But after that, if a turkey just stands out there and keeps gobbling, I move on him."

Most of the time you'll move on a gobbler that you cannot see because of thick foliage or a wrinkle in the terrain. But you should still be careful. Get up and sneak straight back 50 to 100 yards, using brush, trees, a ditch or some other feature to cover your moves. Then make a big, wide circle, evaluating the land as you go and looking for a flat, open chute where a tom might feel comfortable strutting to your calls. If the turkey gobbles as you move, read the call and pinpoint his location. If the bird clams up, blow a crow call. Hopefully he'll gobble and reveal his strutting spot, and then you can slip in close.

Crouch and sneak on your final approach to a bird. If the woods are open, crawl on your belly the last 20 yards to make sure a sharp-eyed devil won't bust you. Set up quickly against a tree and think back to your first setup. Was it yelping on a diaphragm or maybe clucking and purring on a slate that the turkey gobbled at the most? From your new workplace, hit a tom with the kind of calling you know he likes. "Heck," says Salter, "that old turkey should gobble right back, and this time he might walk right into your lap!"

Once a gobbler flies down from the roost, Eddie Salter sits and calls for 25 or 30 minutes. "If the turkey quits gobbling, he's probably henned up or he might have left the area," says the Alabama pro. If you heard another tom gobble nearby earlier that morning, you'd best get up and go hunt him.

◆◆◆◆◆◆◆◆

To fool a wary gobbler, scratch some leaves or pop the brush with a turkey wing to sound like a hen moving around in the area.

him some time to work," says Salter.

At this point, you need to be familiar with some basic spring turkey behavior. A longbeard typically gobbles at a hen call, moves in, stops in an open spot where he can see well, and struts, drums and gobbles some more in hopes of pulling the hot little "hen" (you) out of the brush and to his side. If you call too loudly or too much now, he'll continue to stand out there and strut. But if you tone down, the old boy might get impatient. He's hot to breed and he can't stand it anymore, so he might take a few last steps into shotgun range. Sometimes not calling is a big key to sealing the deal with a tom.

On the other hand, some toms need a little coaxing to cross those final yards. "Call ever so softly, and be discreet," advises Salter. Cluck, purr and make tiny yelps on a diaphragm or slate at the same time a gobbler walks in the leaves or spits and drums. That will make it tough for him to hear and home in on your finishing calls. Hence, you keep him guessing as to your exact location.

Here's a cool trick: If a wary turkey raises the hairs on the nape of your neck by booming a gobble close, keep your composure and come right back at him with a soft little yelp. Then shut up. For icing on the cake, scratch some leaves or pop the brush with a turkey wing. This kind of "comeback" yelp, along with nonvocal turkey sounds, can be deadly when a gobbler is tight.

Worksheet Review

When a turkey thunders on a ridge or down in a swamp or creek bottom, go to him fast. "But before you fill the woods with fancy calling, look around for a flat, open spot to set up," says Salter. "Sit down, be cool and read a turkey's gobbling. Then give him the soft or aggressive calling he wants. Keep reading the gobbler and tone down or be quiet as he comes in."

Heck, with a multi-faceted strategy like that, working a turkey is bound to be a whole lot easier.

THE TURKEY VEST

Every turkey hunter needs a good vest with lots of pockets and a flip-down seat—not just to carry your calls and accessories, but to organize all that stuff.

Let's say a tom gobbles 150 yards away. Slip close, flip down the seat and set up comfortably. Pull your diaphragm case from an upper-right slot in the vest where you always carry it. Need to switch to friction? No problem, dig a slate from the lower-left pocket and pluck its peg from an inner loop. Or grab a box and chalk from the long, thin slot on the side of your vest. Pull a head net and gloves from an inside pocket without thinking twice about it.

See what I'm getting at? Organize and carry your calls and accessories in the same vest pockets and slots on every hunt. The items will be at your fingertips when you need them, and that will help you make all the right moves as a gobbler works close.

Expect to spend $60 to $125 for a well-designed turkey-hunting vest in Mossy Oak or Realtree camouflage. It's money well spent. A good vest even has a flip-out orange cloth. When your work is done, you'll be able to flip out the sash, dangle it over your tom and hike safely out of the woods.

CALLING LONGBEARDS

Ten Advanced Calling Tips

with Chris Kirby

The Expert: **Chris Kirby** of Springville, New York, has the genetics. His father is former turkey-calling champ Dick Kirby, who founded Quaker Boy calls in 1976. Chris called in his first contest when he was five years old. He has gone on to win numerous titles, including the World Turkey Calling Championship in 1995 and the U.S. Open (four times). Today, Chris Kirby, now the honcho at Quaker Boy, is widely regarded as one of the top five turkey callers in the nation. Who better to give us some in-depth tips for fooling the ultimate judges, those long-bearded toms that roam the spring woods?

Here are Chris Kirby's great tips:

1. Vary Your Sound

This is easy with a "cutter" mouth call, like Quaker Boy's World Champ. The call has latex reeds with one corner notched out. To make a clear yelp, slide your tongue into the notch and force air pressure there. For a raspier sound, move your tongue into the middle of the call or over to the opposite edge. "With practice, you can make a lot of different yelps and cutts on a diaphragm like that, and it can give you an edge," says Kirby. "Sometimes switching from a clear yelp to a raspy call, or vice versa, can fire up a gobbler and pull him in."

2. Speak Softly

When you're after a gobbler that has been hassled by other hunters for days or weeks, Kirby advises to be patient and call quietly. "Even if a turkey doesn't gobble back at your first call, resist the urge to scream at him," says

QUICK TIP

◆◆◆◆◆◆◆◆

Most toms roar at least a little as they come to your calls, so you can draw a decent line on their approach. But more birds than you think try to slip in silently. After making a series of calls, ready your shotgun over your knees, keep still and scan the woods. Before moving to stretch or call again, remain still and look for one more minute. That way, you reduce the chances of spooking a sneaker that might be moving in.

◆◆◆◆◆◆◆◆

the New York pro. "Just sit there and cluck, yelp and purr seductively. Stay upbeat and confident. Most of the time a tough old bird is gonna come to soft stuff or nothing at all."

3. Give a Tom What He Wants

"If the judges at the Grand Nationals or the World Championship want soft calls like tree yelps, clucks or purrs, that's what I give 'em," explains Kirby. "If they want louder and more aggressive assembly or lost calls, that's what I do. It's the same with the ultimate judges, those long-bearded gobblers in the woods. If you listen closely and read a turkey's gobbling, he'll tell you what calls to make, and how much and how loudly to call. Some gobblers respond best to soft, plain yelps, while others like excited and raspier calls."

4. Practice Makes Perfect

"As a competitive caller, I have to be perfect on stage, so I practice, practice and practice some more to hit all the right notes and tones," says Kirby. Building, trimming, cutting and tweaking calls have become second nature. All that practice carries over into the woods and gives me lots of confidence when I work gobblers."

5. Diversify Your Call Collection

"To me a mouth call produces the most realistic turkey sounds," says the pro. "But I also know that to impress gobblers, a high-pitched aluminum call or a raspy box with a trilling pitch, like Quaker Boy's boat paddle, is often the way to go. I use friction

In mid-season, look for areas where there is hen activity and you'll locate the longbeards—sometimes three or four strutters!

calls a lot when hunting. They're great for striking gobblers 300 to 500 yards away."

6. Hit the Woods Early

Kirby finds that anywhere in the country, the first couple of weeks of the season are generally the best. "The gobblers' testosterone levels are going crazy, and the birds are pumped to respond to your calls," he says. "Also, gobblers have not yet been bombarded by other hunters' calls. I call a lot and aggressively early in the season. The first half-hour of the morning, I move around and locator-call from high points, trying to find the hottest tom in a tree. Later in the morning I walk ridge tops, yelping and cutting hard, trying to yank shock-gobbles out of toms. Once I find a tom that is gobbling good, I set up and give him what he wants, either soft calls or aggressive stuff. "

7. Go Where the Girls Are

Things are tougher, much tougher, during the mid-season lull, when toms are henned up. Longbeards will give you lots of courtesy gobbles, but they have little or no intention of coming to your calls. "Focus on ridges, flats, fields and other areas with high hen activity because that's where the gobblers will be," Kirby advises. "I often go into one of these areas, set up and listen. If hens and gobblers are close and vocal, I cluck, yelp and cutt fairly aggressively. Sometimes you can rile up a flock of birds and bring them in. But if the turkeys are sort of quiet, I back off and call softer."

8. Late-season Turkey Talk

"I don't mind hunting the last week of the spring season," says the New York guru. "In fact I've done it a lot recently with good success. Sure, some turkeys have been hunted hard. But generally there's a second gobbling peak because the nesting hens won't have anything to do with the toms, and the toms are still fired up. I've had good luck with old gobblers during this phase. Many of them seem to sense that the breeding season is winding down, so they respond well to calls. I use the late-spring leaf cover to move in and set up tightly on a gobbling bird. Then I yelp and cutt fairly hard on either a mouth call or a friction call."

9. Be Patient

Kirby applauds a recent trend among turkey hunters to be more patient, like the old-timers were back in the 1970s and early 80s. "I used to run-and-gun and call a lot, and I still do when conditions are right and birds are gobbling well. But I've also learned to slow down and be more methodical. Now when I'm fooling with a tough old turkey, I might sit for a couple of hours and cluck, purr and scratch in the leaves."

10. Learn Girl Talk

Kirby's last tip addresses one of the biggest mistakes turkey callers make: They don't pay enough attention to hen calls. "I've heard guys sit in the woods and yelp slow or fast for three or four minutes straight. Real hens just don't do that. Listen to as many hens as you can in the woods. Key in to their notes and especially the cadence of their calls. You can also purchase cassettes and videos featuring live hen talk. Keep studying real hens until you can mimic the rhythmic cadence of their yelps. You'll become a much better caller."

Listen to as many hens as you can. Learn to mimic their various calls, especially the rhythm and cadence of their yelps.

TALK LIKE A MAN

On most spring hunts, sweet-talking like a hen is the way to trick a tom. But don't forget that turkeys need a little male bonding every once in a while. Sometimes gobblers shun the girls and hang out together. If you can talk trash with the boys, you'll likely come away with some beards and spurs.

• **The Gobbler Yelp.** Record numbers of toms inhabit farms and woodlands today. Join the chorus using a multi-reed diaphragm, a box call or a glass pot with a wooden striker. You'll sound like a new turkey in the social hierarchy, and another gobbler may come to check you out. This tactic is most successful early in the spring, before the hens are ready to breed.

The main thing to remember when yelping like a tom is to slow down. A gobbler's yelps can be either deep and raspy or fairly clear, but they're always slower than a hen's yelps. Yelp in three- or four-note series, and mix in deep, coarse clucks for added realism.

• **The Gobble.** Gobbling on a rubber shaker or tube call is an excellent locating technique. Loud and attacking, the gobble works especially well for hunting Rio Grande and Merriam's turkeys out West. A gobble at dusk or dawn can set off a chain reaction of gobbling from toms packed into a live oak or pine roost. Back East, if owl-hooting or crow-calling fails to produce, why not gobble once in hopes of shocking the real thing from a tight-lipped longbeard?

You can also gobble to challenge the dominance of an old tom with hens. When you gobble, nearby hens will perk up, and the strutter among them will do a double take and wonder, "Who dares invade my domain?" The bird might roar a gobble to both impress and suppress you. Gobble right back to say you're not the least bit fazed; you're here to stay and looking to steal a few hens. The turkey might lose his cool and run over to kick your tail feathers. Then, of course, you can turn the tables on him.

• **The Fighting Purr.** A few years ago in New York, a buddy and I yelped to a pair of toms that gobbled until they were blue in the face. We went back and forth with the birds for an hour, but they would not budge. Finally, I had had enough. I dug deep into my vest, pulled out a couple of push-peg calls and cut loose some loud, wild, aggravated purrs. The toms boomed more gobbles, broke strut and tore off through the woods, beards swinging! The three-year-old turkeys came within 20 yards, and my pal and I doubled.

The fighting purr does not always produce such dramatic results, but it can work. Carry a set of push-peg calls in your vest. When you pull them out, mimic a knock-down-drag-out fight. Work the friction calls, stop a second to gobble on a tube or shaker, and run the calls some more. Create the illusion of one heck of a turkey fight, and you might bring a tom running.

52

When Gobblers Won't Gobble

with Walter Parrott

Boom or bust pretty much sums up spring turkey hunting. Things are good in March or early April as boss toms, spurred on by warming weather and increasing daylight hours, gobble like mad to gather hens. It's the best time to be in the woods. Traveling widely and booming love tunes, gobblers may trip over their beards as they run to your calls.

Then comes the bust. As longbeards corral more and more gals, the ridges and valleys fall increasingly silent. It makes sense, if you think about it. Mature toms with females at their beck and call have little reason to gobble; they roost with hens, fly down and tread them each morning, and then strut around and breed some more throughout the day.

Here's another thing. Having recently had their tail feathers boxed by the bosses, most of the subordinate two- and three-year-old males are afraid to utter a peep.

Many gobblers will crank back up later in the season, when the hens desert them and go to nest. But for now, times are tough, and it can stay that way for a couple of weeks. So you'd better have a few tricks up your sleeve when toms get a bad case of lockjaw in the middle of the season.

The Expert: **Walter Parrott** of Fredericktown, Missouri, is a key member of Knight & Hale's "Ultimate Hunting Team." He helps design turkey calls and appears regularly on the company's hunting videos and television shows. Parrott has won a ton of state and major turkey-calling championships over the years. He is considered by many to be one of the best, if not the best, yelper in the world today. If anybody can tell us how to make a tight-lipped gobbler talk, it's this Missouri pro.

Run & Gun Strategy

"Most guys can't stand it when turkeys go into that gobbling lull," says Parrott. "They go mobile and get active. They move around and try to find a bird that's willing to gobble."

The Missouri pro says that "running and gunning" is a good idea if you've got several places to hunt close by. "Not every turkey in an area has so many hens that he won't gobble at least a few times, so it pays to hit several spots each morning."

Drive to a farm or woodland at daybreak. Park your vehicle, walk out a ridge and owl-hoot or crow-call. As a last resort, yelp and cackle on a turkey call as the sky turns pewter. If you fail to hear or strike a turkey, motor off to another place and call some more. Cutt and run well up into the morning until you exhaust all your hunting spots.

Running and gunning can also be effective if you hunt big, contiguous country—for example, a tract of public land that sprawls across 3,000 or more acres. The quickest and most efficient way to probe miles of country is to drive the perimeter of the area and stop frequently to call. In a national forest or large state wildlife area, hike logging roads, trails and power-line cuts. "Try to walk hills and ridges, where it's easiest to hear distant gobbles," says Parrott. "When turkeys are in the lull, one or two gobbles are often all you'll get."

There's another good reason for hunting high: Your calls will carry better. When turkeys are tight-lipped you need more shocking power than normal to yank a gobble or two from a bird. Owl-hoot with zest. Blow sharp, aggressive crow calls. Coyote-yip and howl. Later in the morning, once turkeys have flown down for the day, yelp and cutt hard on a diaphragm or friction call.

Be aggressive and versatile. Use your favorite diaphragm, but be sure to toss in some spirited yelps and cutts on a friction device to up your odds. A box, glass or aluminum call with sharp, piercing notes is tough to beat for shocking a gobble or two from a quiet tom.

When toms are henned up and silent, you need to cozy up to them. Call to a bird in the brush 150 to 200 yards away, and he'll probably look your way and explode into strut—but fail to open his beak. But if you happen to

When "running and gunning," call from ridges and hills where it is easiest to hear toms gobble from the valleys and bottoms below.

call within 125 yards of a strutter, he might run out his neck on reflex and gobble, even though he doesn't want to. Sneak along and crow-call, yelp or cutt every 100 yards or so. "No doubt about it, the tighter you are to a strutter, the better the odds that he'll shock-gobble at your call," says Parrott.

When a tom finally roars a response, you've still got your camouflaged hands full. A longbeard with hens may take 30 minutes or an hour to work–if he works at all. "When a turkey is close and strutting, it's generally best to tone down your calls, so the hens won't move away from you and take the gobbler with them," notes Parrott. Cluck, purr and yelp in hopes of enticing the girls and pulling the big boy within gun or bow range.

There's always the chance you'll strike the kind of turkey you're looking for–a two- or three-year-old longbeard sans hens. Be poised to set up in a flash so you won't blow the golden opportunity.

"When you're walking around the woods, you never know when and where a turkey might gobble at your calls, so don't lose your edge," says Parrott. "A bird might rip it just under the lip of a ridge or close in the brush. You've got to be ready."

Always stop in a fairly open area and beside a tree before you call. If a bird thunders close, sit down and set up quickly. "Always wear your gloves and face mask," adds the Missouri pro. "A bird might not gobble much once you strike him, but he might come in fast. You sure don't want to get caught digging in your vest."

Sit & Call Strategy

Roaming and calling all over the woods might not be your style. Or maybe you lease a small area where the run-and-gun strategy is impractical. Perhaps you hunt mostly fields with patches of open timber, where you'll spook a lot of turkeys by hunting too aggressively. No problem. You can trick lock-jawed turkeys with a more subtle approach.

Think back to the scouting you did before the start of the season. Which ridges or bottoms held the most turkey tracks, droppings, scratchings, strut marks and dust bowls? Where did you hear the hottest gobbling two or three weeks ago, when toms gathered hens? Head straight to a place where you know turkeys roost and strut. Even though you cannot hear them, some longbeards are there.

"Think positive," says Parrott. "It's a big part of turkey hunting, especially when birds are not gobbling well. Just because gobblers aren't talking doesn't mean they went anywhere."

MORE TACTICS FOR SILENT TOMS

You may have greater success with one or more of these tactics:

• Set up on the edge of a field or food plot where hens are likely to show up around 9:00 or 10:00 a.m. They may have male company.

• Whether you run-and-gun or sit-and-call, listen closely, and not just for a gobble. You might hear hens clucking or yelping in roost trees, or purring and yelping as they feed. You might hear birds scratching in the leaves. Those turkeys are close, so set up to be ready for any longbeards hanging with the girls.

• Learn what a tom's drumming sounds like and listen hard for the low-pitched call. While a turkey with hens might not gobble much, he'll drum a lot, both in a roost tree and on the ground. Hear the subtle love call, and you know a bird is close—within 100 yards.

• Listen for the tattletale call of a young gobbler. A jake traveling with a longbeard often *keowks* every time the old boy struts for his hens. The call of a jake can give away a gobbler.

• Say you're running and gunning and a jet flies over, a train whistles, a crow caws or a woodpecker hammers a tree. Stop and listen. A turkey might shock-gobble at the sound. If so, move in his direction, set up and start calling.

• As you sit-and-call, toss out a sharp, excited cutt every once in a while. You might shock a gobble from a turkey that is sneaking in. If he's within 125 yards, sit tight and keep up the soft sell. But if the bird sounds 150 yards away or farther, get up and sneak a little closer before calling to him again.

WHY WON'T THEY GOBBLE?

When the April woods turn silent as a tomb, you can take it to the bank that most boss gobblers have hens. But other factors contribute to lulls as well. Nasty weather—high winds, cold rain or even snow—can deaden gobbling activity for a few days. A heavy concentration of coyotes, foxes or other predators (including hunters) in an area can cause turkeys to gobble less than normal, especially when birds are on the ground.

Regardless of what prompts a lull in the gobbling, keep running and gunning in hopes of finally striking up a conversation with a tom. Or sit tight and call in an area with fresh hen sign. Sooner or later you'll make contact with a strutter, and you just might reel him in.

Owl-hoot or yelp from a strategic vantage as the morning sky blushes pink. You might get lucky and make a turkey gobble a time or two. If not, slip into an oak flat, creek bottom, food plot or similar place littered with turkey sign. Hens are apt to show up there sometime during the day with strutters in tow.

"You can't go wrong by playing it cool and patterning turkeys, especially if you've got only one or two small places to hunt," says Parrott. "Look and listen for a couple of days. Try to figure out where the birds go to feed and strut. Go there and set up."

Once there, how much should you call? "I like to slip into a spot where I know gobblers hang out and call every 15 to 20 minutes," adds Parrot. "Mostly I cluck, yelp and purr softly like a feeding or loafing hen."

Sit tight and call for an hour or two or even longer if you have the time and the patience. Many people have the time but lack the self-discipline to tough it out in the silent woods. That is too bad, because the simplest of all strategies makes a lot of sense. Set up in an area littered with fresh sign and mimic a sweet-talking hen looking to hook up, and guess what? Sooner or later a longbeard will strut in to check out your calls. He probably won't gobble much, if at all, so keep still and keep your eyes open.

While the passive technique can work on breeding flocks of gobblers and hens, it is dynamite for fooling satellite or fringe toms. Plenty of these two- and three-year-old birds roam the woods, and they are constantly on the lookout for the chance to slip in and breed a hen.

Satellite toms keep their distance from boss birds, and they may gobble only once or twice in the morning, if at all. But they will come to your calls. "Set up in a good, open spot against a tree where you can see all around—even behind you," says Parrott. "A gobbler is apt to come in silently from any direction. Again, have your gloves and face mask on and be ready."

Level your shotgun over your knees as you cluck, yelp and purr. Listen for a tom's subtle drumming; you can hear it for 100 yards on a still day. Listen for turkey feet shuffling leaves. Sit still, and scan the woods and foliage. One day you're bound to get lucky and spot the tip of a fanned tail...a flash of crimson...a head big and white as a softball... and then the beard of a giant strutter!

Take a deep breath and pull the trigger. Cut loose a mighty yell as you race out to claim your trophy. Now it's time to make a lot of noise, because whacking a tight-lipped tom is a huge accomplishment.

Why Do Turkeys Do That?

with Bill Jordan

Listen in as two guys set up on a gobbler one morning:

"What do you think that old devil's gonna do?" one hunter whispers.

"Well, yesterday he flew down and strutted up this ridge," his buddy responds.

"So he's gonna do that again this morning?"

"Who knows? He might keep gobbling and come up here again. Or he might pitch down, shut up and go the other way. Heck, that turkey doesn't know what he's gonna do five minutes from now."

How true! Wild turkeys are wildly unpredictable,

and that adds yet more intrigue to the spring hunting game. But toms high on testosterone and hens pining for love do have some tendencies. Let's focus on ten common questions about turkey habits, and follow up with tactics that will help you score when they do what they do.

1. Why do toms gobble hard on the limb, fly down and then head off away from my calls?

These days when you hear a boss bellowing at dawn, there's a darn good chance he is roosted

The Expert: **Bill Jordan** of Columbus, Georgia, needs no introduction. The creator of the Realtree and Advantage camouflage patterns is one of the most recognizable faces in the hunting world today. Jordan, host of the *Realtree Outdoors* television show, is best known for chasing trophy whitetails across North America. But hunting wild turkeys in the spring—and solving some of the riddles of the intriguing game—is another of Jordan's outdoor passions.

with hens, as well as one or more subordinate toms. Most mornings the turkeys fly down, mingle and then march away from your yelps. Why should they make the major effort to come over to you? The longbeards already have hens, and they strut off behind the girls to a feeding or nesting area. The subordinate males tag along.

"You've got a couple of options in this situation," says Jordan. "You can try to circle the turkeys and get in front of them, or you can remain at the roost site."

Most of the time Jordan moves on the birds, but he admits that sometimes sitting tight and listening has its advantages. As a morning wears on, the mature toms have all the fun, breeding the hens and bullying the lesser males. After an hour or so of abuse the subordinates—not just jakes, but many of them two- or three-year-olds with ten-inch beards and good spurs—give up and start looking for other options. "If a turkey hears you calling back at the roost site, sometimes he'll return and start gobbling," says Jordan. "Listen and watch for a gobbler working back to you."

2. Why do turkeys gobble well one morning but go silent the next?

I liken it to a college football team—say, Nebraska. One Saturday the Huskers are pumped and play their hearts out, leaving it all on the field. But physically and mentally drained, the players may have a hard time getting up for their next game.

Likewise, one day toms might gobble like crazy, fly down, breed hens, fight and expend a ton of energy. The next morning the gobblers are spent, so the woods are quieter.

From a hunting perspective, here's what it means. Say you hear six or seven toms bellowing long and hard on a ridge one morning. Well, expect to hear only two or three birds gobbling there the next day. The gobbling you do hear might be far less lusty than it was the previous day. But on the bright side, you know at least six toms are in the area.

"Try to work the one bird that gobbles the best," advises Jordan. "If that doesn't pan out, set up on a nice, open ridge and call awhile. Maybe set out a couple of decoys. With all those gobblers in the area, one might strut to your calls. Be ready, because he might sneak in silently."

3. Why do hens shun my calls one day, but yelp and cutt back aggressively the next?

I believe a hunter's calls pose no threat to hens early in the breeding season, when the gals won't accept the gobblers anyway. Clucking, yelping and cutting, you're just one of many turkeys roaming the woods. Hens go about their business and ignore your calls.

But things change when the peak rut rolls around. Mature hens that hang with old gobblers don't like the calling competition you throw into the mix. Agitated, they often yelp and cutt back as if to say, "Quit all that sassy talk!" If you fire back yet more heady yelps and cutts, a boss hen is apt to turn tail and walk away, taking her gobbler with her.

"When gobblers are henned up and breeding, don't call too aggressively to the hens," Jordan advises. "Instead of trying to fire up the girls, tone down and try to pull 'em in with clucks and yelps. A lot of times a strutting turkey will follow."

4. Why do gobblers roar at one type of call (or one hen's yelping), but blow off other turkey sounds?

All of us sound differently. While one person's baritone voice might appeal to you, another person's shrill speech might grate on your nerves. It's much the same with turkeys. A tom might fold his tail feathers and shun raspy hen talk–or he might run out his neck and triple-gobble at a high-pitched call.

"That's why you should change your calls," suggests Jordan. "If a turkey won't gobble much at a mouth call, switch to a box or a slate. Try two or three different hen sounds. Sometimes even a little thing like changing the pitch or tone can make a big difference."

5. Why do two or more gobblers often march side by side to my calls?

Go watch a bunch of Realtree's turkey-hunting videos. Amid all the action and tips you'll notice something interesting. On probably 70 percent of the hunts, not one but two, three or more gobblers–sometimes jakes and longbeards, but often all longbeards–came walking or strutting to the hunters' calls. It verifies the "fringe gobbler" phenomenon I've been writing about since the early 1990s.

Years ago boss toms simply ran off the few inferior males that tried to hang around them. But with record numbers of gobblers in many areas today, dominant birds would have to spend all spring challenging subordinates. The bosses would rather strut around and procreate with hens. So they relent and let lesser toms hang around the perimeter. Typically, the subordinates don't gobble much, if at all.

Keep that in mind each time you set up on a turkey. The raucous gobbling you hear likely comes from a dominant bird. But there's a darn good chance that one or more inferior toms are in the area. "Listen closely and keep your guard up," suggests Jordan. "Be ready for a second or third gobbler to sneak into your calls."

6. Why won't a gobbler cross a fence or creek to get to my calls?

Turkeys walk, hop and fly across fences, creeks, ditches and canyons every day. So why won't they cross an obstacle to come to your yelps one April morning? Well, I'll let you in on a little secret. Many times they will come over.

In one memorable hunt from Realtree's *All-Stars of Spring IV* video, a hunter ran across a hard-gobbling Rio in Texas. A tall woven-wire fence separated hunter and bird, but the guy didn't have time to maneuver and take the obstacle out of play. So he backed off from the fence, sat down and started yelping and cutting. The turkey gobbled, waddled across the pasture and flew the fence. The hunter dropped him at 25 yards.

"You can't always set up on the same side of a fence or creek with a turkey," notes Jordan. "If that's the case sit on the opposite side and give a gobbler your best calling. If he's hot enough, he might come on over."

7. Why is it that an old gobbler won't come to my calls one day, but the next morning he runs in?

I believe a boss–we're talking about a tom three to five years old–is going to show interest in your

Why does an old gobbler hang in his roost tree well after daybreak some mornings? Because he can sit up there and see well for hundreds of yards in all directions. He looks primarily for hens flying down in the woods, but he is also alert to predators moving around. So once you sneak in and set up in a spot, sit tight. Watch and listen for the old boy to fly down. Once the bird is on the ground, then shift your setup if you need to. The tom will be less likely to see you.

◆◆◆◆◆◆◆◆

Some gobblers run to decoys while other toms shy away from them. Still, most of the time it doesn't hurt to set out a fake or two, especially when hunting around a field or other open area.

calls maybe four days out of the season. "All those other mornings, two big things work against you," says Jordan. "Either a gobbler doesn't want to come to where you're set up, or the bird has hens."

Well, to make the most of the few good mornings, recognize when it's a bad day and back off. Say one day a tom is roosted alone in a thick creek bottom. He gobbles at your tree, yelps and flies down, but he won't come to you through the brush. Oh well, slip out of the area and leave him alone.

Suppose you come back the next day and find the gobbler roosted in a better spot—but then you hear hens yelping all around. You can try to call in the girls, but they might turn and take the tom away. Again, leave.

By backing off and not pressuring an old turkey, you up your odds of killing him when conditions are finally right. One morning you might come back and find the tom roosted solo on a nice, open ridge 200 yards from that thick bottom. "Make one call and the bird might pitch down and run to you," suggests Jordan.

8. Why do some turkeys run to decoys while other birds run away from them?

Filming hunts across the country each spring, Team Realtree relies heavily on decoys. "We use 'em to pull turkeys close to the camera," says Jordan. "I can't tell you how many times we've had gobblers run 200 yards across a pasture to get to our decoys. We've filmed birds attacking decoys and trying to breed them."

But occasionally the opposite happens. Sometimes a gobbler will spook and run away from decoys. More typically, a turkey might spot a fake hen, strut to within 50 to 75 yards of it and hang up. After a while, he realizes the decoy is not going to walk over to him and he turns and leaves.

Each bird is different, so you never know. "But most of the time it doesn't hurt to set out a decoy or two, especially when hunting around a field or other open area," adds Jordan.

9. Why does a tom gobble and approach my calls, only to hang up 60 to 80 yards away?

You're probably dealing with one of two types of turkeys: either a two- or three-year-old bird that has been pressured by other hunters, or a truly ancient, sharp-spurred sultan that has played the mating game many times before. Either way, the tom commits only so far to your calls. He then stands out in a safe zone and gobbles and struts, hoping to pull the hen (you) out of the brush and to his side.

Should you keep calling? "Each situation is different," notes Jordan. "Go with your gut feeling as to how much to call to a hung-up turkey. If a tom is gobbling hard, you can generally call a lot and fairly loudly. When a bird is not gobbling much, you probably ought to tone down."

Sometimes not calling is the best way to break a bird your way. Bite your tongue and sit tight. Let the turkey gobble and gobble, and gobble some more. "Every once in a while, reach out and scratch leaves, like a hen milling around," says Jordan. "If the turkey is hot enough, he might get impatient and strut those last 20 to 40 yards into shotgun range."

10. Why does a gobbler often quit gobbling and slow down as he commits those final yards to my calls?

Some 60 to 80 yards out, an old turkey often quits gobbling and switches to drumming, his close-range call to a hen. He might take a step, explode into strut, drum, drop his tail, crane his neck, look around, take another step…you get the picture.

When a turkey clams up and goes into closing mode, many hunters get nervous and think something has gone terribly wrong. Then they mess up the situation by calling too loudly or moving too quickly, and end up spooking a bird that they had already fooled!

"You've got to remember that an old turkey takes his time coming in," says Jordan. "When he quits gobbling, be patient and sit still for 20 minutes to even an hour. Look hard and listen closely for drumming sounds. That gobbler ought to show up soon."

TOTAL TURKEY CAMOUFLAGE

Bill Jordan and the folks at Realtree offer these tips on turning invisible in the turkey woods:

• Unlike deer and other mammals, wild turkeys can see and assimilate color, so wear camouflage head to toe.

• Match your camo to the environment you hunt. For spring turkey hunting, a green pattern is a good choice.

• Hide the movement of your face and hands with camo gloves and a facemask.

• Your bow or shotgun moves more than anything else, and at the most critical moment of a hunt. Cover an old shotgun with camouflage tape to hide reflections and disguise movements. Or use a new gun or bow with a camo finish.

• Turkeys have an awesome sense of hearing, so wear soft, quiet garments. Napped-cotton camo is great in the spring.

• Don't "skyline" when walking and calling, or especially when approaching a gobbling turkey. No matter how good your camouflage, a turkey might see your silhouette against the sky. Always "sidehill" along ridges and walk close to cover, which maximizes the effectiveness of your pattern.

• Don't "spotlight" by setting up in sunshine. Choose a spot next to a tree, in the shade or mottled shadows.

• Most of the time you won't notice an animal unless it moves. And most of the time a turkey won't see you unless you move at the wrong time. Good camouflage can help hide mistakes. It's best to remain still, though, and move slowly and at the right time during a turkey hunt.

The Toughest Toms

with Ronnie "Cuz" Strickland

"One of these evil spirits can wreck your home life, your job and your general well-being. He'll screw up your entire spring season if you let him."

Strickland is talking about what southerners call a "bad turkey." No matter where you live, you probably know the type. The bird roars a little or a lot on the limb each morning. He flies down and gobbles a little or a lot more. For a while the tom might bellow at your calls, and he might even strut a few yards in your direction. As you sit white-knuckling your shotgun and craning your neck, looking for his crinkly white head in the brush, the old devil gobbles—300 yards away! Then he is gone. A turkey like that probably has a grin creased across his beak as he whips your butt day after day. "No doubt about it, a bad turkey gets a lot of fun out of your misery," muses Strickland.

As the mornings pass, the hunt for a bad bird turns from fun to work to obsession. You pull your best moves and setups, and give the bird your finest yelping. He booms gobbles, hundreds of them, but refuses to come your way. You try decoys; he thumbs his beak at them. You switch gears and challenge him with fighting-gobbler calls; if a turkey can laugh, he busts a gut and runs the other way. After a week or so of such nonsense, you can hardly eat or sleep. You go through the motions at work. You're

The Expert: **Ronnie "Cuz" Strickland** of West Point, Mississippi, is one of the most recognizable folks in the turkey-hunting world. A man with a big laugh and a wonderful sense of humor, Strickland has appeared in many videos over the years, and he's a star on the seminar circuit. He is a vice president of Mossy Oak camouflage, and executive producer of the company's *Hunting the Country* television show. Strickland has a passion for butting heads with the toughest toms. "A bad turkey is a bad dude," he says, "but he can be had."

Approach a "bad" turkey from different directions and angles each day. Then set up and call in fresh spots until you finally fool him.

grouchy at home. All because of a 20-pound turkey. Why put yourself through it?

"It goes to the core of the sport," says Strickland. "It's just what it's all about. When you finally call in and shoot a bad turkey, it doesn't get any better than that."

Who Is the Bad Boy?

The orneriest gobbler in an area is three or four years old, and he's bad to the bone for a couple of reasons.

The first is pressure. The harder you hunt an old tom, the tougher he is to trick. The turkey might look down from his roost tree and see you moving in, morning after morning. Your calling, fine as it is, can turn a bird leery after a few days. And chances are you're not the only one after the evil spirit. One day while you're at home or work, another hunter might bust the bird off the roost. Some dude might even sail a load of No. 6 shot over the bird's white-capped head.

"Most bad turkeys are not as smart as hunters think," notes Strickland. "They are just scared to death, most

likely from one too many encounters with lead."

Hens make a bad boy even badder. An old turkey gobbles on the roost each morning to rally his gals. When he flies down, two, four or more hens pitch down to him. The longbeard might gobble at your calls, but with all those girlfriends at his side, why should he strut 100 yards or farther to check you out?

Most hunters naturally assume that the toughest tom in the woods is a bull of a bird, a 20-plus-pounder with a beard as thick as a paintbrush. Well, that's not necessarily so. The baddest turkey I ever called in and killed weighed a mere 16 pounds; his beard consisted of a few coarse, squiggly strands. Old birds lose weight and rub their beards thin as they tread hens in the spring. They are lean and mean, with awesome spurs, more than an inch long and sharp as box cutters.

All this adds up to lots of character!

Hunting Strategies

"With a bad turkey you've got to get out of calling mode and go into hunting mode," says Strickland.

"If a tough gobbler came to every sweet yelp he heard, he wouldn't be a tough gobbler for very long. Form a battle plan. Learn the areas a gobbler likes and then try to pattern his moves."

Let's say a gobbler shuns your calls a couple of mornings in a row. Instead of moving around, calling like mad and pressuring the bird even more, sit back, shut up and study the old devil. Listen to his gobbles as he walks off, and try to determine where and how far the turkey goes to strut for the day—maybe a field, oak flat or shady creek bottom. Somewhere over in that direction is where you should hunt the following morning.

Many people fall into the trap of approaching a gobbler from the same logging road, field edge, creek bottom or other convenient path each morning. A wise old bird probably smiles all over himself as he patterns your moves. You ought to mix things up. Circle around and go to a gobbler from a different direction. Then set up and call in fresh spots. Vary your approaches and setups enough, and you might finally end up in a spot where a turkey thinks, "Hmm, I've never heard a hen over there before. Maybe I ought to check her out."

It's generally best to approach a tough gobbler cautiously. After all, calling to the old devil from 125 yards away is better than blundering in, spooking him and ruining yet another hunt. Strickland agrees, but with one notable exception. "The close-in setup is one method that can work like a charm. If you can spot a gobbler and his hens late one afternoon, maybe in a field or food plot, sneak close and watch or hear where the turkeys fly up to roost. The next morning, before daylight, get aggressive. Try to sneak in and set up below the birds, as close as you dare inside of 100 yards."

In tight, you eliminate at least some of the calling competition from hens. And sometimes the gals will help you out. If they fly down and start calling all around you, the gobbler might unknowingly pitch down into your lap.

"This is a tough call and requires the perfect situation," Strickland warns. "You might get away with spooking a hen or two off the roost, but if you alert the gobbler to your presence, all bets are off and the hunt along with it. But sometimes you just have to go for it to outsmart an old bird."

Calling Techniques

For days or weeks, you and other hunters have yelped like crazy at a bad turkey, without a sniff of success. So why not tone it down? "Try to refrain from calling very much, and don't get too loud or too wild," says Cuz. "Try clucks and purrs, and switch between mouth and friction calls."

That said, Strickland cranks it back up when things work out and he gets a super-tight setup. "If you can set up within 100 yards of an evil spirit at daybreak, try calling more than normal and while the hens are still in the trees. That aggravates some hens. Once they fly down, they might come to check you out and bring an old gobbler with them. If you get a lead hen fired up with your calling, keep it up. Mock her calls and don't let up."

On all those mornings when a tom hits the ground, gathers his hens and marches defiantly away from your calls, try, well, nothing. Leave the bird alone. Slip out of the woods and go get a cup of coffee. Maybe take a nap. Sneak back into the woods at 10:00 or 11:00 a.m. and try to raise the gobbler with a crow call, or a mighty yelp or cutt on a turkey call.

Your odds are better than 50-50 that a bad turkey will shock-gobble at your call. And you know what? He just might come! "Late in the morning some, most or all of a gobbler's hens might have left him," says Strickland. "If this is the case, an ornery turkey might trip over his beard running to your calls. Hunting late in the morning, or even in the afternoon where it's legal, is one of the best ways I know to fool a bad bird."

The Janet Ridge Gobbler

To dupe a tough turkey you've got to dig deep—real deep—into your bag of tricks. Scratch leaves with a stick as you call to mimic a hen moving around. Every once in a while try purring aggressively like two toms fighting. At daybreak flap a turkey wing (or your cap) in the leaves to sound like a hen flying down.

Strickland was introduced to the latter trick one morning 25 years ago, light-years before most of us had heard of "winging it." The tale of that hunt epitomizes the wonderful obsession that is hunting a bad bird.

"I hunted this Mississippi gobbler nine days in a row," says Cuz. "Nine days in a row he whipped my butt. The turkey would gobble three to five times on the limb every morning, but never when he hit the ground. He had hens, lots of 'em."

Strickland had the gobbler within 50 yards three times and saw him once. "He looked small and black as the bottom of a dry well," he recalls.

With four days left in the 1978 season, Strickland stood outside his hunting camp, milling around and wondering just how in the world he could get that turkey. The man who owned the neighboring farm stopped by for a chat. "I told him about the gobbler, and he smiled," says Cuz. "The fellow was around 65 years old, weathered but in good shape and laid back. He listened intently and finally said, 'Boy, you want to kill that turkey? Then go get a line on where he goes to bed.'"

Strickland went out and roosted the bird that evening. "I went over to Mr. Olin's place and told him about it. He asked if he could come along the next morning, and I said sure. Our plan was set."

In the silvery dawn the hunters slipped up Janet Ridge. Day cracked and the turkey gobbled. Mr. Olin took over. He put out his pipe and put his finger to his mouth, motioning for Cuz to keep quiet and follow.

"I couldn't believe how close we sneaked to that turkey," remembers Strickland. "We sat down, and after what seemed like hours, Mr. Olin pulled out an old stiff cloth and flapped it wildly. I jumped and thought he was nuts! The flapping rag did sound like turkey wings, but at the time I had never heard of the trick."

The gobbler roared. Strickland longed to yelp, but Mr. Olin motioned for him to keep still and quiet. "The turkey flew down and walked within 20 yards of me," Cuz says with a laugh. "I was so shocked I almost forgot to shoot. But I regained my composure and whacked that turkey. He had long spurs and a thin, 11-inch beard. He weighed all of 15 pounds."

The gobbler was jet black and looked unlike any Eastern turkey Strickland had seen before. "Mr. Olin said the turkey was one of the old breeds the Indians used to hunt. I don't know about that. But I do know I was almost sad driving home, knowing I wouldn't have that bad gobbler to hunt anymore."

BACK OFF!

When an old tom gobbles like mad but won't come in, a flustered hunter generally does one of two things. He sits yelping and cutting for 30 minutes or more in hopes the bird will finally break his way. Or he takes off on a wild run to a new setup, where he sits and hammers the gobbler with yet more calling. Once in a blue moon that aggressiveness pays off. But most of the time you'd do better to play it smart and cool.

Most people believe that once a turkey clams up and walks, he goes a mile or farther. Not so. An old Eastern or Osceola tom generally doesn't move very far. He might just drift off a few hundred yards and hang in a strut zone for the rest of the morning. Now, a Merriam's or Rio Grande gobbler is a different critter. He might take off traveling over hill and dale, so you'd better move with him.

But let's get back to an ornery old Eastern or Osceola tom. What happens when you try to move on him? That's right, the turkey is apt to see you and spook. And you know what that means. He'll be harder to call up the next day.

Speaking of calling, what gives when you continue to pound away at a tom, either from your first setup or after moving to a second spot? Well, remember the bird probably didn't go far once he quit gobbling. He'll stand out

there and strut, listening to all that high-octane yelping and cutting. After awhile he'll get leery. Again you've schooled that turkey and made him tougher to call.

No matter how hot a turkey sounds, some mornings he simply won't work. The bird might have hens with him. Maybe you're set up on a ridge or flat where he doesn't feel comfortable coming in. For whatever reason he'll stand out there and gobble and gobble hoping you, whom he perceives to be a hen, will come to him.

My advice: Back off, especially when dealing with a "bad bird." For starters, when you sneak away and leave a turkey alone, you know he didn't see you. Also, you gain an advantage by not hammering a tom and educating him with your calls. In short, when you let a gobbler go about his daily routine of strutting and breeding hens with no hint of pressure, you're better off in the long run.

You can pretty much bet the turkey will roost and gobble somewhere close the next morning. Come back, set up in fresh digs and begin the game anew. Now the gobbler might be ready to work. His hens might have left him overnight. Or he might like the looks of the new ridge or flat where your calls are ringing out. Get your gun up and yelp. That bad tom might trip on his beard as he motors in for a look.

The Myth of the Call-Shy Turkey

with Ray Eye

Back in the 1970s and 80s turkey hunters were tough. On all those mornings when gobblers shunned their calls and strutted off in the opposite direction, the old-timers took it like men. They knew it was just part of the game.

We modern hunters are more thin-skinned and sensitive. If we yelp two or three times and a longbeard won't come a-running, we start looking for justification and even vindication. "That dang turkey is call-shy" is one of our best excuses on all those mornings when gobblers whip our butts.

Well, guess what? According to Ray Eye, there is no such thing as a call-shy turkey.

"I can't count the number of times over the past few years that hunters have told me that," says the Missouri pro. "I've even heard people say a gobbler knows the sound of a particular type of diaphragm or box call, so you'd better not use that.

"Turkeys are sharp, but c'mon, they can't reason like that. You can't tell me a gobbler stands out in the woods, listens to our calls and thinks, 'Hmm, that's not a hen, that's a hunter, I'd better go the other way!'"

Eye may not believe that gobblers get call-shy, but he's convinced they do get people-shy in the spring. "On popular hunting grounds, turkeys see and hear trucks and ATVs in the timber most every day," he says. "Birds sit on the roost and see hunters walking around, silhouetted on ridges and sloshing through creeks. They get bumped off the roost and spooked in their strut zones."

Eye thinks all that pressure, not some learned aversion to calls, is what makes some old turkeys less prone to gobble and less apt to work into shotgun range.

Attitude Adjustment

Eye believes you're doomed if you go into the woods thinking you're hunting a call-shy tom. "You don't have confidence that you can kill a turkey," he says. "You are so worried about spooking a bird that you set up too far away from him. You call too softly and infrequently, and with no spirit. When a gobbler won't come to your three or four little yelps, your fear has been confirmed. But he's not call-shy. It's just that your uninspired calling has wrecked your chances."

Well, an attitude adjustment is in order. "Forget about all that call-shy stuff you might have read," says Eye. "Go in and hunt even the toughest turkey with a positive attitude. Don't be afraid to move in tight on him. Yelp and cutt aggressively, within reason, and you might kill that bird."

QUICK TIP

❖❖❖❖❖❖❖

When hunting a public area, check a topo map or an aerial photograph for out-of-the-way ridges and creek bottoms. Try to get away from roads and other hunters to where you can have fun and hunt safely. "If you strike a turkey in a remote spot, there's still a good chance he's been pressured some, but he's not call-shy," says Eye. "Yelp and cutt like you normally would and sound like a hen ready to hook up with a gobbler. You can get him."

❖❖❖❖❖❖❖

The Expert: **Ray Eye** of Hillsboro, Missouri, is one of the best-known turkey hunters in the world. He was winning calling contests and shooting gobblers back in the 1970s, when turkey hunting was not as popular as it is today. Eye has shown remarkable staying power. Today he continues to be a popular seminar speaker, and he is one of the most quoted turkey-hunting experts in magazines. Eye is always quick with a laugh and some awesome quotes, especially when it comes to tricky topics like "call-shy" turkeys.

BLIND LUCK

The hunter who moves in tight and yelps like a hen hot to breed is the one who fools the "call-shy" turkeys.

To keep gobblers from becoming "people-shy," Ray Eye limits the trucks and ATVs that rumble through the private properties he hunts and guides on in spring and fall. He often uses blinds, either elaborate commercial models or simple strips of camo mesh or burlap stretched between two trees.

"The farms I hunt in northern Missouri have lots of pastures and crop fields dotted with woodlots and draws," he says. "If you walk around and call too much in open country like that, all sorts of turkeys will see you and run or fly off. Too much of that can change the birds' patterns. That's why I hunt from blinds a lot. You can slip into a good spot before daylight and sit and call for hours. Eventually you'll see turkeys, but they won't see you. Using blinds puts a lot less pressure on gobblers."

In the spring, Eye erects blinds 100 to 200 yards off known roosting spots. He also sets hides on the edges of fields where gobblers go to strut and gather hens. A high, open ridge between a roost and a field is another great place for a blind.

Eye uses blinds in October as well. "In the fall turkeys get people-shy in a hurry too," he says. "Try setting a blind 100 to 150 yards off a ridge roost, between the roost and a crop field, oak flat or other feeding area. Slip into the hide before daylight, sit down and begin calling without being seen. When the turkeys fly down and start making their rounds, you can often call in a couple of birds or even a whole flock."

One morning a few years ago, Eye drove around a farm in northern Missouri, prospecting for turkeys. The landowner rode shotgun and told him, "Ray, we've got a bunch of birds up here, but they're call-shy as all get out. If you yelp too hard or cutt at them, you'll spook 'em." Eye listened and nodded.

Around 9:00 a.m. Eye parked his truck, got out and cutt on a box call. Two gobblers roared down in a creek bottom. Just then two of Eye's buddies from Arkansas drove up. Eye cutt again and the birds gobbled again.

"You boys want to hunt those turkeys?" Eye asked as the hunters grabbed for their vests and guns. "Just remember, they're call-shy as all get out."

The hunters slipped into the bottom, set up close to the birds and began yelping and cutting like banshees. The landowner cringed. Eye grinned. Pretty soon two shots rang out and back came the

Here are a few more ideas for better success, according to Ray Eye:

• When turkeys won't talk, set up in an area with lots of fresh sign, one where you heard turkeys gobble earlier in the season. Start calling softly and then get more aggressive. Sit still, look and listen, and be ready for a gobbler to sneak in silently. If a turkey doesn't respond or approach your setup after 45 minutes to an hour, move quietly 200 to 300 yards and call again.

• Stake decoys in field edges and clearings where they are easily seen by turkeys. Hen decoys work best late in the spring season, when most hens are nesting and gobblers are looking for company.

• Every calling situation is different. However, a good rule of thumb is to set up within 100 yards of a gobbler, on the same level or slightly above him. It's best if no big obstacle—creek, deep draw, whatever—is between you and the turkey. Start calling softly at first (toss out three or four yelps and clucks) and see how the bird responds. If the turkey cuts you off—that is, if he gobbles while you yelp—pause and then call more aggressively. If he gobbles again, lay down your call, keep quiet and make the gobbler come look for you. If you don't see him after 10 minutes or so, call again, more aggressively.

• Sometimes we think too much and make turkey hunting more complicated than it really is. Gobblers do what they want! One day a turkey might pitch down a hill. The next morning he might fly up a ridge. You never really know. Just set up and call in flat, open spots where it is easy for gobblers to come to you.

• When a turkey is on the ground and gobbling down in a draw or maybe on the backside of a ridge, walk straight to him. Shuffle leaves and snap twigs along the way. As you close the gap, slow down and creep as close as you dare. Now you've got the gobbler wondering if a hen or another gobbler is walking nearby. The bird doesn't know, because humans and turkeys walk with the same "clump, clump, clump" of two feet. When you finally stop and sit down, the gobbler might be ready to come and check out the first call you make.

Arkansans, a pair of 24-pound longbeards slung over their shoulders.

"Ray, y'all got any more of these call-shy turkeys we can hunt tomorrow?" one guy asked with a laugh.

Summary

Think about it. Which hunter is a gobbler most apt to come to? The guy or gal who sets up 150 yards away from a turkey and yelps softly and tentatively three or four times? Or the hunter who moves in tight and yelps and cuts like a hen hot to breed?

"I'll take the latter approach every time," says Eye, "and I'll kill my share of turkeys. But even on all those mornings when a gobbler shuts up and struts away, I don't make any excuses. An old turkey whipping your butt is just part of the game."

From the Stage to the Woods

with Steve Stoltz

A major calling competition like the Missouri Open or the National Wild Turkey Federation's Grand Nationals is a sight to see. And, of course, it's a hoot to hear! To impress a panel of finicky judges, the best callers on the planet put on a wildly entertaining display of clucking, yelping, purring and kee-keeing. The camo-clad guys and gals are so into it that for a few minutes in the spotlight they seem to morph into hens, preening, bobbing and strutting around on stage amid the props of hay bales, trees and stuffed toms. The audience eats it up.

As you might expect, most of today's top competitive callers are excellent turkey hunters as well. So naturally one might ask a couple of questions. Do contest callers cluck and yelp the same way in the woods as they do in an auditorium? Or do they change their calls and calling routines when hunting for beards and spurs? Well, let's find out.

Similarities & Differences

"For me, calling is all about rhythm, whether I'm on stage or in the timber," says Stoltz. "Getting the rhythm of a hen down pat is the way to score with both judges and gobblers." The only way to perfect your rhythm is to practice and then practice some more.

The big difference between competitive calling and the real thing is the pressure. "The competition is so good on stage these days that you simply cannot afford to make a single mistake in a major calling contest," Stoltz says. "I mean, not one. Just one little slip on a yelp or a kee-kee will cost you a spot in the finals and some big money."

A competitive caller also must have a solid and well-choreographed program. From the tree yelp to the kee-kee to the assembly call of an old hen, Stoltz practices his presentation over and over for weeks and months. Although the calls that contestants are required to make differ from contest to contest, the stage yelper needs a routine and a presence.

"But there's no routine or program in the woods," notes Stoltz. "Every hunting situation and every turkey you run into are different, so your calling should vary all the time. Heck, if you've got a routine, your woods calling is probably in a rut."

Fortunately, perfectionism isn't at home in the woods either. Some live hens are rough, squawky callers. They sound terrible, as if their mouths are full of gravel. Sometimes even clear, sweet-calling hens make mistakes, peppering their yelping sequences with off-key whines and squeals.

"A judge may cringe if a competitive caller hits a bad note, but a hunter can't spook a turkey by making a mistake," notes Stoltz with a laugh. "And if you do mess up, just roll right over it with more yelping and clucking. The great news is that these 'mistakes' often fire up toms and make them gobble even more."

QUICK TIP

❖❖❖❖❖❖❖

The best thing about becoming a competitive turkey caller is that it gives you confidence. On stage you have to be perfect, so you practice, practice and practice some more with your calls. That will give you a boost when you work finicky old toms.

❖❖❖❖❖❖❖

The Expert: **Steve Stoltz** of St. Louis, Missouri, is a firefighter by trade. He moonlights as one of the top competitive turkey callers in the nation. Stoltz has won numerous state and national calling titles, including the World Championship in 1993 and the Grand National Champion of Champions in 1998. Stoltz, a member of the Drury Outdoors video team and a pro-staffer for Outland Sports, is also an awesome hunter. Here he gives us some perspective on turkey calling from the stage to the woods.

When Steve Stoltz yelps, hens turn green with envy. But the Missouri pro is the first to say there's a whole lot more to tricking toms than just fancy calling. Here are his top 5 timber tactics:

• **Know your area.** Get out and walk your hunting areas before the start of the season. Read the lay of the land as you scout for tracks, droppings and feathers. When turkeys start gobbling in the spring, pinpoint where they roost. Try to pattern where the hens go to feed and where the gobblers strut later in the day. The better you know your ground and the gobblers that live there, the easier it will be to set up and call 'em in.

• **Hunt where gobblers will go.** Turkeys always take the path of least resistance. Say a gobbler is ripping it down in a draw. One side of the draw is rough and steep, while the other side slopes gently up to a field or oak flat. If you were a gobbler looking for a hot hen, which way would you go? Always set up and call in a nice, open spot where it is easy for a turkey to come to you.

• **Get in the buffer zone.** When the conditions are right and the turkeys are hot, a tom might come tearing in as he runs to your calls from 150 to 200 yards out. But during most phases of the breeding season, and especially in the peak when gobblers are henned up, it pays to get into the "buffer zone." Before you make a call, try to sneak within 75 yards of a gobbler if you can. Use cover, a ditch or maybe the crest of a ridge to get in super-tight. An old turkey with hens, or maybe a tom that has been pressured, might not come 100 or 200 yards to your calls. But he'll strut 40 or 50 yards to check out your soft clucks and yelps.

• **Roost toms.** Get out in the evening and try to roost a turkey or two whenever you can. When a turkey gobbles at your owl hoots or crow calls and gives away his tree, you'll know where to start hunting the next morning. A lot of times you can sneak into a gobbler's buffer zone and set up in the dark. Heck, the turkey might be in shotgun range when he flies down. Try to call him in before he moves off with hens for the day.

• **Hunt new ground.** If you're having trouble getting a turkey, go to a new area. You and other hunters might have moved around, called too much and burned out your first spot. Sometimes a change of scenery is all it takes to call in and whack a longbeard.

Now for someone like Stoltz who isn't prone to mistakes, the big question is this: Do your calls sound different in the woods than onstage? "I tend to call with a higher pitch when hunting because I've found that many if not most turkeys like high-frequency yelps and cutts," he says. "Calling competitions are indoors, where the acoustics of rooms vary from flat to echoing. Inside, I believe that lowering the pitch of calls gives me better realism."

Calling Devices

Most competitive callers make their own customized mouth diaphragms. They experiment with various latex and prophylactic reeds and aluminum frames. They tinker with all sorts of fancy reed cuts, splits and notches. In short, they clip, bend, stretch and cut until they find that one magical call that sounds more like a turkey hen than a turkey hen herself!

Stoltz's competitive call is a spin-off of a four-reed diaphragm with an inverted V-cut that he invented. "If I build 100 mouth calls based on this design, one call might sound right for the big stage," says the Missouri pro. "But you know what? Any of those 99 rejects would be fine for the turkey woods. It goes back to that margin of error. A mouth call for competition has to sound perfect, but you can get away with a lot less perfection and more of what I call 'turkey sound' in a woods call."

Stoltz is one of the best mouth callers in the world, and he obviously uses a diaphragm a lot when hunting. "A diaphragm is perfect for 75 percent of hunting situations," he says. "It's a versatile call that you can use for excited yelping and cutting, or soft clucking and purring. I like the high frequency of yelps and cutts I get from it. A mouth call also leaves your hands free to hold and move your shotgun or bow."

Stoltz also knows that switching over to a friction call can pay off big-time in the woods. "When I'm trying to strike or fire up a turkey, I often go to an aluminum call or a box call. They might not score with human judges," says Stoltz. "But they can sure fool longbeards."

If you're toying with the idea of entering a turkey-calling contest you ought to heed the advice of Stoltz, one of the top money winners on the major calling circuit the last few years.

"For starters, learn to sound like real turkeys," he says. "Buy audiotapes and videotapes of nothing but hens in the wild, clucking, yelping, purring, kee-keeing and doing their thing. Spend as much time as possible in the woods and listen to hens. Then master the mouth call. The key to winning or placing in any contest is not to mimic another caller, but to sound like the real McCoy."

Go to as many state, regional and national competitions as possible. "Watch, listen and videotape the action," suggests Stoltz. "Then go home, study your tape and pay particular attention to the calling styles that are consistently winning."

If you see Stoltz, Walter Parrott, Chris Kirby or any of the other top callers at a competition, don't be afraid to go up and ask for a few pointers. "Most of us are eager to help out up-and-coming callers," says Stoltz.

At some point you've got to get your feet wet. "Enter as many local and state contests as you can," encourages Stoltz. "And don't be afraid to jump into a regional or national contest. It will be great experience, and the more experience you get, the more successful you'll be on the circuit."

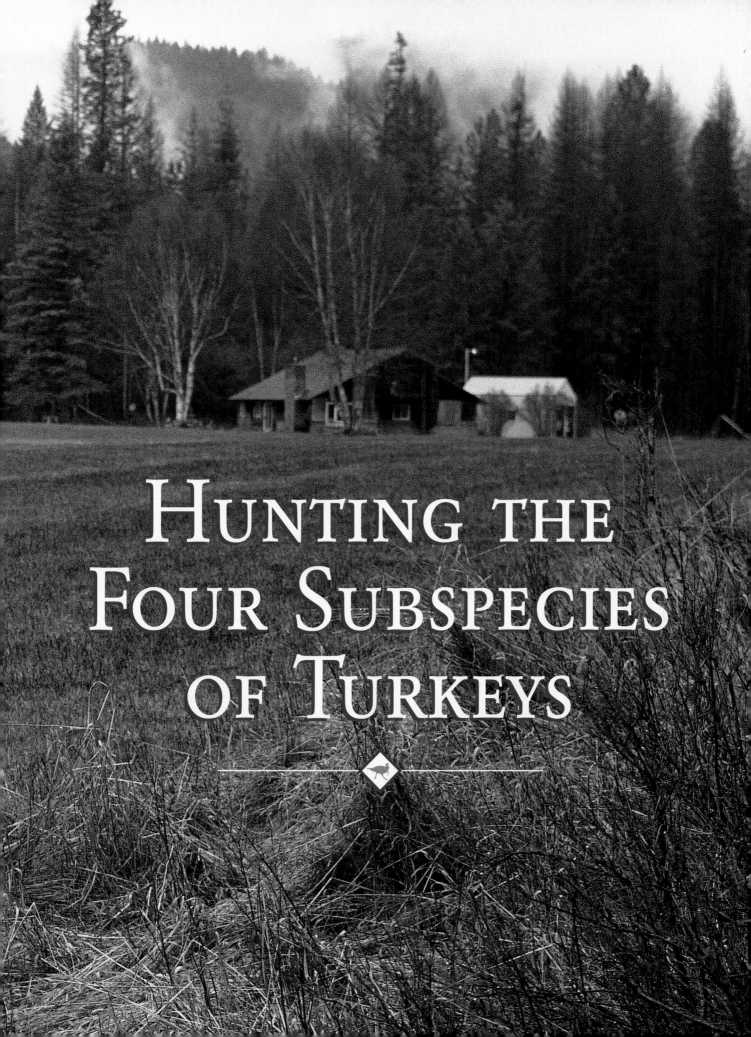

HUNTING THE
FOUR SUBSPECIES
OF TURKEYS

The Phases of Spring

with Harold Knight

Let's say you grew up chasing Eastern turkeys in the hills and hollows near home. Over the years you've hunted like a wild man and honed your skills. You've become a darn good hunter who tags a couple of longbeards every spring. You still plan to hunt your home state, of course, but you're looking for new challenges.

One March you jump into your truck and drive south for a crack at swamp gobblers in Alabama or Mississippi. Or maybe in April you head west to Missouri or Iowa, or out to Texas for a rendezvous with the Rio Grande subspecies.

Whatever your destination, you're stoked when you arrive in new turkey country. But after a couple of days things start to go sour. You don't hear many birds gobbling. The toms that do roar on the roost hit the ground, clam up and run away from your calls. A week later, tired and frustrated, you head home with a pocketful of unfilled tags.

"Those turkeys don't act right," you mumble on the long trek back. "Danged if I could figure 'em out!"

"I hear stories like that all the time," says Harold Knight with a chuckle. "Most of the time the problem was that the hunter didn't have a clue what phase the turkeys were in when he went to hunt them."

According to Knight, the behavior of

The Expert: Thirty years ago **Harold Knight** was a barber in his hometown of Cadiz, Kentucky. He teamed up with long-time friend David Hale, and they began making turkey calls in a basement workshop in their spare time. In 1984, with business booming, Knight hung up his scissors and began making tube and friction calls full time. The rest, as they say, is history. Today, Knight & Hale is one of the premier game-call companies in America. And Harold Knight is widely regarded by his peers as one of the most insightful turkey hunters on the planet.

One April morning, Harold Knight and I called to a tom for half an hour. The bird thundered back but wouldn't budge. "Let's go," my friend whispered. We got up and sneaked all of 50 yards, to a spot where the woods opened up into a beautiful, glistening flat. "I bet that turkey will come here," Knight whispered as we floated a second volley of calling. Five minutes later the tom came strutting and gobbling, putting on a grand show until my shotgun roared. The moral: Sometimes when you move on a turkey, you don't have to go far.

◆◆◆◆◆◆◆◆

hens and toms changes, sometimes quite dramatically, during five transition phases in the spring. To be successful you need to understand what's up with turkeys during each phase, and then key your tactics accordingly.

To help you do it, Knight and his buddy Hale put their heads together, drew upon a combined 80 years of turkey-hunting experience and developed their *Gobbler Guide.* "The guide will help you hunt better anywhere in the U.S. and during any phase of the spring breeding season," says Knight. Here is just a sampling of *Gobbler Guide* wisdom.

Phase 1

WHEN: March 5 to 20 in Zone 1 (from South Carolina to Texas to southern California and all points south); March 20 to April 4 in Zone 2 (from North Carolina to southern Pennsylvania and west to central California); April 4 to 19 in Zone 3 (northern states).

BIRD BEHAVIOR: Turkeys begin to break out of winter mode. Large flocks of toms and hens travel together, and their movement is fairly predictable. Toms gobble mostly on the roost. Hens are very vocal, yelping and cutting. Gobblers strut behind the hens and sometimes fight.

TACTICS: As you slip close to a roosted flock, keep in mind there is not much foliage in the woods yet. Gobbles carry a long way, so turkeys are probably a little farther away than you think. Once you're in tight, set up and call softly, gradually increasing the volume of your clucks and yelps. "Use several calls to sound like several hens," suggests Knight. "Try to rile up an old hen. She might come to you and bring a gobbler with her."

During the midmorning hours, use a crow call or a shrill hawk whistle to locate strutters. Try the "fighting purr" call to mimic two toms fighting. "All that racket can make a turkey gobble," adds Knight.

Be ready for possible snowy conditions in a northern or Rocky Mountain state. But don't worry about it. Toms will still gobble, strut and breed hens during a freak spring snowstorm.

One of the best times to hunt is late in the spring, when the hens are nesting. Lovesick toms travel widely and thunder gobbles, making them susceptible to your calls.

Phase 2

WHEN: March 20 to April 4 in Zone 1; April 4 to 19 in Zone 2; April 19 to May 3 in Zone 3.

BIRD BEHAVIOR: Big flocks begin to break up. Gobblers compete for hens. You'll often find a dominant tom with several hens, and perhaps a subordinate gobbler or two. Hens start to lay eggs, but they return to the gobblers each day. Expect lots of gobbling at dawn, but then an early-morning lull as hens and toms breed. Subordinate turkeys looking for hens often start gobbling after 9:00 a.m. or so.

TACTICS: "Midmorning is the best time to hunt," Knight says. Crow-call and hen-cutt to locate gobblers, especially the lonely subordinates. Try to get within 100 yards of a gobbling bird before calling. Hens still call aggressively, so you can too. Cutts and raspy yelps tend to work well. Once you've got a turkey going, be patient and tone down your calls. "He has to quit gobbling and strutting and start moving toward you," notes the Kentucky pro. "By not calling very much, you can force a turkey to do that."

Phase 3

WHEN: April 4 to 19 in Zone 1; April 19 to May 3 in Zone 2; May 3 to 18 in Zone 3.

BIRD BEHAVIOR: Most hens are now on their nests. Lonely toms gobble hard and stay on the roost longer each morning. Mature gobblers become somewhat territorial: They hang in comfort zones where they can see predators and be seen by other turkeys. The few hens that are still receptive to breeding leave the toms quickly each morning.

TACTICS: "It's like the peak of the deer rut and the best time to hunt," says Knight. Sneak tight to a roosted tom, but don't call until he flies down. Then fire him up with aggressive clucks, yelps and cutts on a diaphragm or friction call. "After that, wait him out, yelp softly and make him come to you," adds the Kentucky pro.

At midmorning, try to shock gobbles from birds with cutting calls or crow calls. Try to find the comfort zones where old gobblers strut. "Find such a zone and you'll increase your odds of calling in a gobbler," says Knight. "Try setting out a jake decoy with a hen as you call in one of these areas." Knight goes on to say that afternoon hunting, where legal, can be awesome now.

Phase 4

WHEN: April 19 to May 3 in Zone 1; May 3 to 18 in Zone 2; May 18 to June 3 in Zone 3.

BIRD BEHAVIOR: Breeding begins to taper off. Gobblers spend a lot of time in strut zones where they have called up hens in the past, especially on ridge points and around fields where hens nest and dust. A gobbler will often strut in one spot for 10 to 15 minutes before moving on to another zone in search of the last available hens.

TACTICS: Try to pattern a tom by his "walking gobbles" as he moves between strut zones. But don't call too much, if at all, until you get a good setup in a flat, open strutting area. "Try to wait until a gobbler is walking to you in his zone before calling," says Knight. "Use soft clucks and feeding purrs while scratching in the leaves. Remember, a gobbler wants to see a hen before he approaches, so call sparingly."

Hunt around fields, clear-cuts and other hen-nesting spots; toms may strut nearby. "By now most gobblers have been pressured by hunters, and hens are not very vocal, so that's another reason you ought to tone down your calling a bit," says Knight.

Phase 5

WHEN: May 3 to 18 in Zone 1; May 18 to mid-June in Zones 2 and 3.

BIRD BEHAVIOR: Gobblers begin to get back together and go into their summer/fall mode. Expect sporadic but sometimes intense gobbling. Toms re-establish pecking orders, so fights may break out again. In some areas poults hatch. "Turkeys spend a lot of time feeding and loafing in and around green fields," notes Knight.

TACTICS: If the tag end of your season is still open, set up around fields and stake out decoys. "Try gobbler clucks or jake yelps on a tube or friction call," says Knight. "And give the fighting purrs one last shot. Remember, gobblers are looking for male company now. But don't overcall, because turkeys are not all that vocal late in the season."

GOBBLING MESSAGES

As you hunt the five phases of the turkey rut, listen for hidden messages in the "love tunes" of longbeards.

"These days when a turkey **roost-gobbles** like crazy, I figure he sees or hears a hen in a nearby tree," says Harold Knight. "He's trying to gobble her in, and if he does, he'll fly down with that hen and shut up. How many times has that happened to you?"

Slip in tight, inside 100 yards of a roosted tom, and set up. "Your best chance is to get close early and try to call the gobbler away from the hen," says the Kentucky pro.

Suppose it's 10:00 a.m. You stroke a high-pitched aluminum call. *Gaaaarrroobble*— 300 yards away! Well, before you pump your fist and get all excited, you'd better test that bird a couple more times.

"Move a little toward the turkey and yelp or cutt again," says Knight. "If the bird doesn't answer two or three more times, he isn't hot and he probably won't work. He just gave you a courtesy or shock gobble the first time around. You can pretty much bet he's strutting with hens. You'd better keep looking for a hot turkey to hunt."

You yelp, and a tom fires back **break-in gobbles** that cut off your calls. "That gobbler is red hot, and you should be able to kill him if you don't screw up," notes Knight. "Sit tight— don't try to move on a turkey like that—and keep calling. Give him what he likes, whether it's yelps on a diaphragm or raspy friction calls. A turkey that breaks in on your calls should come pretty fast early in the season. It might take him awhile longer later in the spring."

Now let's say you yelp, and 10 to 20 seconds later a tom gobbles. It goes on like that awhile, with a bird giving you more **delay-gobbles.** "That turkey is not all that excited, but at least he's interested," says Knight. "He might be a pressured bird, or more likely he is saying, 'I've got hens over here, come on over if you want.'"

If you think you're dealing with a pressured bird, sit tight and call softly for a while. Scratch leaves to mimic a hen moving around. The bird might eventually break and come.

However, when hens are in the picture, "a turkey that delay-gobbles to your calls will generally walk off after awhile," notes the Kentucky pro. "He gave you the chance to come on over, but you didn't, so he lost interest and left.

"You might as well get up and move on that turkey. Flank him or, better yet, circle in front of him and call. He might think a hen is tagging along with him. At some point the turkey might get interested and come on in."

Another scenario: You yelp, and a turkey roars close. You dive for cover, set up and call again. The bird thunders 50 to 100 yards farther away! The more you call, the farther the turkey sounds, his **walking-gobbles** growing fainter.

"That tells you one of two things," says Knight. "Either the turkey has a hen and she is dragging him away from you, or the bird is alone but traveling to a strut zone that is in the opposite direction of where you are calling."

Get up and go. No way are you going to turn that turkey around with calling. "Move quickly to a nearby flat, ridge point or field," says Knight. "Set up, call and hope the gobbler shows up there to strut."

Say it's noon. You hear a turkey gobbling every now and then, maybe every 5 to 10 minutes. If a crow flies over and caws, he shock-gobbles. If a hawk whistles, he roars. Sometimes the bird answers your calls with a **random-gobble,** other times he doesn't.

"You can bet that turkey is strutting with a hen," says Knight. "He's just more vocal than most strutting birds. The good news is that he gives away his location."

Slip in and set up. "But don't do what 90 percent of hunters do and hammer the bird with yelps or cutts," warns the pro. "If you do, his hen might take him away. Instead, make a few soft clucks, purrs and yelps. The turkey might drift over for a look."

Every once in a while you'll strike gold and run across a tom gobbling hot and heavy late in the morning. According to Knight, that turkey might be **panic-gobbling.** "A turkey is all blown up and strutting for hens," he says. "Suddenly he looks up and the hens are gone. Maybe they slipped away to feed or to sit on their nests. Well, the turkey panics and starts gobbling. He's lonesome and looking for the hens. He's red-hot and easy to call."

A frantic tom might respond to fancy calling, but Knight plays it safe. "Slip in close, set up, get your gun ready and make a few little clucks and yelps," he says. "That turkey might think, 'There's one of my hens!' He ought to run in for a look."

HUNTING THE FOUR SUBSPECIES OF TURKEYS

Hunting the Osceola Wild Turkey

with Terry Drury

On a road map of Florida, draw a line from the city of Jacksonville in the east to the mouth of the Suwannee River in the west, and then go south to the Everglades. This is where you'll find the pure strain of Osceola wild turkey–some 100,000 of them. Osceolas are named after the famous Seminole chief who led his tribe in a bloody border war with the Americans in the early 1800s.

Due to this restricted range, relatively few of America's 2.6 million turkey hunters go for an Osceola each year. "Those of us fortunate enough to hunt the Florida turkey find a striking bird," says Drury. "I'm forever amazed at the beauty of an old swamp gobbler."

A streamlined version of the Eastern turkey, a mature Osceola tom weighs an average of 16 to 18 pounds in the spring, though a 20-pounder is not uncommon. Bathed in morning sunlight, the gobbler's ebony feathers spin iridescent reds, blues, golds and greens.

"Check out an Osceola's wing feathers. They're distinctive," notes Drury. The wing primaries are mostly black with narrow white veins, and that sets the bird apart from the other subspecies.

An Osceola tom's beard drags the ground, but it is often thinner than an Eastern turkey's. Wading the swamps and walking on sand, a Florida tom

The Expert: **Terry Drury** of Bloomsdale, Missouri, is executive producer and co-host of the popular hunting videos from Drury Outdoors. Each spring the die-hard turkey hunter travels around the country, rolling tape and calling in longbeards. Florida is one of Drury's favorite spots; he never misses the opportunity to head south and duel an old swamp gobbler. Drury offers his tips and tactics for hunting the Florida, or Osceola, subspecies, which is typically the capstone of a turkey hunter's grand slam.

SWAMP GEAR

Osceola
Turkey
Range

0   100   200
Miles

Use the same shotgun, load and calls in Florida as you do anywhere else. But you'll need some other gear to hunt safely and effectively:

• Wear knee-high rubber boots when wading through swamps. Leather snake boots lined with Gore-Tex are a good choice, since you never know when or where you might run across a snake in a swamp or pasture.

• Temperatures will be in the 70s, 80s or maybe even the 90s, even when the season opens in March, so wear lightweight cotton camouflage.

• Swamps breed mosquitoes. If you hunt in Florida without a can of DEET-based repellent in your vest, you're crazy. Before a hunt, mist your pants and shirt, and really coat your cap and gloves. Reapply bug dope several times each morning.

• A swamp is flat and thick. All the moss-laden trees and pockets of black water look the same. You can and will get turned around every once in a while. Carry a map and a compass or a GPS unit to find your way out.

•Use a small flashlight when wading into a swamp and setting up in the dark. You sure don't want to step into a creek channel over your head or sit on a snake! Point the light's beam toward the ground and you won't spook turkeys.

• A small, aluminum-and-mesh seat is great for hunting a swamp. You can set up virtually anywhere without getting your butt wet.

does not rub off the tips of his spurs. To the contrary, he grows long, curved, sharp hooks, which are prized by hunters.

Where to Hunt

Many wildlife management areas in central and southern Florida offer spring turkey hunting. You ought to check one out. "I've hunted several public areas over the years, and the hunting there was pretty good—better than I expected," says Drury. "It was a challenge, and it really gave me a taste of what Florida turkey hunting is all about.

"On most public grounds, the swamps are huge, flat and thick, and hunting Osceolas requires wading through a lot of black water. You can bet you'll be on the lookout for snakes and gators," Drury adds with a chuckle.

Gobblers in these swamp areas often strut and gobble on humps of dry ground only six or eight inches high. Getting to the birds before they quit gobbling each morning without them hearing or seeing you is tough. "All in all, if you kill a big Osceola on public ground, you've earned it," says Drury.

If this soupy terrain is too much for you, you're better off hunting private lands. Without question, the best Osceola hunting is found on private cattle ranches in the lower two-thirds of Florida. These ranches offer prime turkey habitat: a mix of cypress swamps, improved pasturelands and oak hammocks. The birds typically roost in the swamps, fly down to the pastures at dawn to feed and strut, and retreat to the shade of the oak hammocks when the sun rises high into the sky each day. Generally you can hunt and call in the pastures and hammocks without stepping into a swamp and getting your feet wet.

While the hunting on private lands is great right now, how long will it last? That question concerned both Drury and me the last time we hunted together in Florida. We had permission to hunt a 1,000-acre ranch just north of Tampa. In the wee hours of opening morning, traffic on the drive out had been heavy. Housing developments, resorts and strip malls lined the highway. When I floored a longbeard at dawn, golfers were just teeing off on a new course a mile away. I wonder if some guy flinched at the sound of the shot? Drury whacked his tom a couple of hours later, while thousands of tourists were pushing through the turnstiles at Busch Gardens and Walt Disney World less than 50 miles away. Amidst all the hustle and bustle of the Sunshine State, how long could the ranch and its turkeys survive?

"I don't want to sound too negative, because the turkey hunting is tremen-dous on many Florida ranches right now," says Drury. "But no doubt it is getting tougher and tougher to find private land to hunt. Residential and commercial development will contin-ue to take a lot of the best turkey habitat. If you know somebody down there who has a good place to hunt Osceolas, go now."

Hunting Tactics

As a rule, Osceola toms don't gobble as much as their Eastern kin. And you've got to remember this: When a bird gobbles from deep in a cypress swamp, he always sounds farther away than he really is. "The flat, thick swamps soak up the sounds of a turkey's gobbles," notes Drury. "You might hear a gobbler and think he is 400 yards off, when he's really roosted only 200 yards away. You've got to approach a turkey carefully. If you bust off toward a bird too fast, you might walk right over him and spook him."

In a public swamp, wade toward a gobbling bird as best you can. But when hunting a ranch, lay back a little

Ranches with improved pasturelands and swamps are the best places to hunt a boss bird in Florida.

Osceola toms can be called into your setup; as a rule, though, they don't gobble as much as Easterns do.

bit. Set up on the edge of a pasture, or in the head of an oak hammock that juts out into a field, 150 to 200 yards from a tom. Set out three or four hen decoys, along with a fake jake. At first light the tom will sail from his cypress roost and alight in the pasture to strut and gather hens. If he hears your calls and sees your decoys, there's a good chance he'll strut over for a look.

Late in the morning, when the angry sun rises and singes their feathers, turkeys retreat to swamps and oak hammocks, where they hang out for the day. Though the birds are largely inactive and silent, it pays to stay on the move and glass the edges of cover. You might spot a strutter loafing in the shade, like Drury and I did one day a couple of years ago.

"I thought I heard a turkey gobble over there a couple of times earlier that morning, but I wasn't sure," recalled Drury. "Down there, coursing faint gobbles is always tough. But I kept at it until I pinpointed his whereabouts."

We took off on a flanking assault, circling to the left and rear of the strutter, and set up on the edge of a swamp 150 yards away. As Drury and his cameraman settled into their positions, I whispered, "I'm gonna hit him with a call. Watch his reaction."

I yelped once on a box.

"He stuck out his neck and gobbled," Drury said, though none of us could hear it.

"I'm gonna yelp again," I replied, fingering the lid of the call.

"Uh, I wouldn't do that," said Drury, digging his face into his gun stock. "He's coming on the run!"

The gobbler waddled into view, beard swinging, but he kept running left. Just as I fixed to cluck and turn the bird, he figured out that he'd overrun the "hen." The turkey broke back to the right, walked in, ran up his neck and stared back into the brush at us. It never ceases to amaze me how a gobbler can hear just one call and home in on it from 100 yards or farther away. Drury's shotgun roared and the bird went down.

Calling Tips

One morning in western Florida I hunted with John O'Dell, another member of the Drury Outdoors video team. We sneaked within 200 yards of a gobbling tom, staked out a few decoys on the edge of a pasture and sat down. The sky turned metallic silver and the old boy flew down. "He's on the ground. Pour it to him," O'Dell whispered.

Hmm, strange. Years ago a grizzled old-timer who lived in a cabin down in the Everglades had taught me to cluck and yelp softly to an Osceola, and that is what I had always done, with some success. But on this morning I said, "What the heck?" and followed O'Dell's lead. As he yelped and cutt on a mouth call, I chimed in with clucks and yelps on a glass call and then a box. It was a calling orgy not often heard down in Florida, I suspect. The horny gobbler liked it, roared and moved closer.

I scanned the pasture. Wisps of fog rolled in and out, playing tricks on my eyes. I would see the turkey coming, and then he would vanish. I'd spot him again, then he was gone. Finally the fog lifted and there, at 30 yards, stood the strutter like a grand apparition. Shivering, I pressed the trigger and bagged my best Osceola ever. The bird was heavy and wore an 11-inch beard and 1½-inch hooks.

"Yeah, I have heard people say you shouldn't call too much in Florida," says Drury. "But I've found that if you hit the timing of the breeding season just right, you can call aggressively to an Osceola gobbler, just as you can to an Eastern or a Rio Grande. If you catch a turkey hot and ready, he'll respond to lots of yelps and cutts."

Drury adds this caveat: "As a rule, though, Osceola toms don't gobble as much as Easterns do. When you set up on a turkey that is not gobbling all that great, start him off with soft calling. Take his temperature. If he likes low-key clucks and yelps, keep giving them to him. I've shot several Florida toms that came to just one or two little calls."

THE NWTF: WORKING FOR THE WILD TURKEY

When you thrill to the gobbling of an old tom in Florida, or anywhere else in the country for that matter, you owe a lot to the National Wild Turkey Federation. When the NWTF was founded in 1973, there were an estimated 1.3 million turkeys and 1.5 million turkey hunters in North America. Over the past three decades, the NWTF staff and its corps of dedicated volunteers have worked tirelessly with state and provincial wildlife agencies and corporate partners, and those numbers have grown at an astonishing rate.

The NWTF has spent hundreds of millions of dollars on over 20,000 projects that have expanded the ranges and increased the populations of all the turkey subspecies. Today, approximately 5.6 million wild turkeys inhabit 49 states and a couple of Canadian provinces, and 2.6 million people hunt for longbeards.

The NWTF is growing fast, with nearly a half-million members in 50 states, Canada and 11 foreign countries. It is quickly becoming one of the most respected and influential pro-hunting conservation organizations in the world.

Everyone who reads this book should join the NWTF, and enlist their friends. The NWTF is working for the wild turkey and your rights as a hunter. Check out their website, www.nwtf.org.

Six, seven million turkeys? Three, four, five million turkey hunters? Thanks to the NWTF, those numbers are on the horizon.

Vagabonds of the West

with David Blanton

Your coyote yips scream in the chilly mountain air. An *obbblle* floats a long way through the ponderosa pines. You set off in that direction, sliding down slopes and huffing up ridges, zeroing in as the tom's roost-gobbling grows louder and louder. Pumped and sweating a river, you set up on the edge of a meadow, catch your breath and eke out a tiny tree-yelp.

Not one but four toms bellow! Grinning as dawn oozes from silver to gold in the high country, you yelp a bit louder. The turkeys thump down from their roosts. You ready your shotgun, grin some more and wait.

HUNTING THE FOUR SUBSPECIES OF TURKEYS

Just then the quartet roars again—200 yards out and going hell-bent in the opposite direction! Frantically, you dig a box call from your vest and cutt. You can barely hear the birds' last gobbles as they race up and over a mountain.

It can happen like that out West. Merriam's and, to a lesser degree, Rio Grandes are the vagabonds of the turkey clan. Some mornings the birds seem to lace on track shoes and sprint out of their roosting areas. This behavior adds intrigue and more than a little frustration to the chase.

"One thing's for sure: When the turkeys start going on a line, you're not gonna stop or turn them around with calling, no matter how good you are," says Blanton. "Sometimes the more you call, the faster they run. If they see you, they might go up and over a mountain, like elk do."

The Expert: **David Blanton** of La Grange, Georgia, is executive producer and co-host of the *Realtree Outdoors* television show. Each spring the longtime turkey hunter travels across the United States in search of exciting and unique adventures to bring his viewers. Many of Blanton's most memorable turkey hunts have occurred out West, in the big, beautiful country that the Merriam's and Rio Grande subspecies call home.

Why They Run

Like most turkey addicts, you probably grew up hunting birds in small to mid-size woodlands in the East or South. Well, the first time you venture west, the enormity of the turkey habitat will both amaze and excite you. From Texas and New Mexico up to Montana and the Dakotas, you can chase gobblers on plains and mountain slopes tens of thousands of acres across. "The country is awesome—big, beautiful and wide open," notes Blanton. "You'll take one look at it and think, 'How in the world can I call in and shoot a turkey out here?'"

The larger and more open the habitat, the farther any game travels. One morning you might find a flock of Merriam's birds roosted and gobbling like mad in a canyon. Go back the next day and that spot might be quiet as a tomb, because the turkeys are roosted in a canyon or in an oak grove two or three miles away.

Hens might partially explain why westerners roam so widely and seem to run from your calling. "In the spring many old Merriam's and Rio Grande gobblers travel with hens—lots of 'em," says Blanton. "A lot of the old hens hate it when you call. The more you call, the faster the hens move away, and the gobblers go with them."

Scouting the West

The hunter who heads out West should plan on at least two days of scouting. This is especially true when planning a do-it-yourself adventure on a sprawling national forest or Bureau of Land Management tract. But even on private land with an outfitter or ranch manager to tell you where flocks hang out, you should still get out and see for yourself where turkeys roost, feed and strut.

"Topo maps and binoculars are a must," says Blanton. "One exciting thing about hunting the West is that turkeys are so visible. You can drive for miles and spot gobblers all over

the place, usually with hens." Of course you'll also glass a lot of big country with no turkeys in it. That's good too, because it helps you narrow down the best spots to hunt.

In the Southwest, many Merriam's turkeys inhabit elk country. The birds wander in canyons, meadows and 6,000- to 8,000-foot mountains during April and May. The turkeys almost always roost in ponderosa pine trees. Check your topo map for preferred roost sites on north- and east-facing slopes near creeks. The turkeys fly down to strut and feed in canyon bottoms thick with Gambel oaks.

Farther north in Wyoming, Montana and the Dakotas, Merriam's roost in cottonwoods or yellow barks, and toms strut in adjacent grasslands and meadows. In eastern Nebraska, the easternmost range of this subspecies, you might find hens and gobblers traveling the hardwood forests with their Eastern kin.

Rio Grande turkeys inhabit the plains. In Texas they roam ranchlands dotted with live oak trees, mesquites and cacti. In Kansas and Oklahoma, the birds live in draws and grasslands with scrub oaks and cedars.

Good roosts are sometimes few and far between on the plains. Scout for tall oaks, cottonwoods or sycamores along rivers and streams. Beneath those trees you are apt to find a mother lode of tracks, feathers and droppings. "In Texas you can sit in a grove of live oaks at dusk and have 50 or more Rios fly up all around you, yelping, cackling and gobbling," says Blanton. "It's pretty awesome, and you sure know where to hunt the next morning."

Rios are apt to strut anywhere in their open habitat. Check out a crop field or cattle pasture near a creek or river, especially if there's thick nesting cover for hens nearby. Scout for tracks, droppings and strut marks in sandy ranch roads. When the sun rises each day and shimmers on the plains, glass for strutters in the shade of oak or cottonwood trees.

Texas Rios flock together in large numbers. Trying to call gobblers away from all those hens is a challenge.

In the hot and arid West, both Rio and Merriam's turkeys sometimes visit creeks, stock tanks and other water sources in late afternoon. Pinpoint the blue areas on a topo map, and check them for fresh tracks, droppings and strut marks.

Hunting & Calling Tactics

On any given morning a flock of Merriam's turkeys might pitch down from their pine roosts and mix and mingle awhile, or sail 300 yards down into the bottom of a canyon. Deciding where to set up is always a crapshoot, but as a rule, think high. "Most of the time that will put you in good calling and maneuvering position," says Blanton.

Anytime you can set up on or near a hillside thick with oak brush, nuts, seeds and other dining pleasures, do it. Hunt Merriam's turkeys (or Rios for that matter) that roost near a food source, and you're in good shape. The hens will pitch down and feed at dawn; the toms will strut around the gals and peck some, too. Since the turkeys are not wont to beeline for a faraway feeding area, they are less prone to shun your calling and run. To the

contrary, a gobbler might like the sound of your yelps and want to investigate.

One thing you'll love about Merriam's and Rios is how they love to gobble, especially at dawn and dusk. While they will bellow at the same barred owl hoots and crow calls you use on Eastern turkeys back home, your best bet out West is a coyote call. "High-pitched yips, barks and howls really turn those turkeys on," notes Blanton. An elk bugle also works great for locating Merriam's toms.

When an Eastern tom roars deep in the timber, his gobbles seem to rattle the ground. When a Rio or Merriam's tom gobbles out in the wide-open spaces, he sounds like his head is stuck in a can. "Don't let the acoustics of the country and those faint gobbles fool you," Blanton warns. "A western gobbler is usually closer than he sounds, especially on a windy day. And it's almost always windy when you hunt out West."

When you do get a tom hot and bothered and gobbling at your calls, keep them up. If you tone down or quit calling to a western turkey, he

Western toms love to strut near rivers and creeks. Find water, and then hunt and call nearby.

tends to lose interest and walk away. Now don't blow a gobbler off a hillside or out of an oak motte with loud, fancy calling. Just keep clucking, yelping and purring seductively till he struts into shotgun range.

Many mornings a flock of Merriam's turkeys will fly off the roost, hit the ground and march over a steep mountain or fall off into a deep draw. If you can't follow the birds quickly, let them go. You can waste all morning chasing toms that run and gobble in inaccessible places. You'd be better off driving a mile or so to a valley or series of ridges and hills that you know from scouting holds more birds.

Some days, however, the terrain is hospitable. You can use the contours of ridges, points and canyons to flank and circle a vagabond flock.

One morning years ago in Wyoming, Blanton and his buddy Brad Harris hunted a Merriam's tom that hammered on the roost. "The bird flew down into an opening, but he didn't pay our calling any mind," recalls Blanton. "We slipped over a ridge, glassed the turkey and saw why–he had 12 hens with him."

The turkeys moved off into a canyon, and the hunters flanked and followed. They called every once in awhile, and now and then the tom would gobble and strut into view. "As the morning wore on, the turkey began to lose his hens," says

Blanton. "After two hours, he was down to six hens. By 11:00 they were all gone. We slipped out a ridge, set up and made one call. The turkey ran in gobbling and we got him."

The Georgia boy learned a lesson that day. "If you can hang tough until a gobbler loses his hens you're in good shape," he says. "When a western gobbler is alone in the spring, he'll run a mile to your calls. It's pretty amazing.

"Keep circling and glassing and keep tabs on a gobbler until you end up in a good spot to call him in. A lot of times a Merriam's gobbler will stay on the move for hours, but he won't go all that far. He'll just strut up and around and back with his hens. It took us all morning, but we shot that Wyoming gobbler pretty darn close to where he had roosted."

Rios can be worked just as you would hunt Eastern turkeys. If you can slip undetected into a patch of live oaks or cottonwoods one morning, go for it. Set up within 100 yards or so of a roost and give the turkeys a few tree clucks and yelps to let them know you are there. Crank up your calling once the turkeys fly down.

Unlike Merriam's, Rios tend to hang around awhile beneath their roost trees. Hens preen and peck for feed while toms strut, gobble and tread a gal when they can. "If you feel good about your setup, sit tight and continue to call in hopes a gobbler will break away from his hens and come in," says Blanton. "If the turkeys eventually drift off toward a feeding or nesting area, get up and try to cut them off at the pass."

To Blanton, the midday hours are best of all out West. "Early in the morning most of the gobblers have hens, but later in the day, many of those hens are long gone. As I said, when the gobblers are alone, they will run a long way to your calls."

But first you have to find them. Drive or hike ranch roads and glass for toms strutting on the plains or in canyon bottoms. Blow a crow call, and yelp and cutt on a turkey call. "A loud, high-pitched box call carries a long way and is my choice for shocking gobbles out of turkeys," notes Blanton.

All-day hunting is legal in most western states, and it pays to hang tough in the field throughout the day. "Cover lots of country and call aggressively, and you might strike a gobbler anytime," says Blanton.

In late afternoon, head for a canyon or an oak grove where you know turkeys sometimes roost. If there is a creek, stock tank or other water source in the area, great. You might catch turkeys grabbing a drink before they head to bed.

If dusk falls and you've neither seen nor heard any turkeys, hit a box call and then a coyote howler. If a Merriam's or Rio Grande gobbler is anywhere near, he'll answer, and his gobble is apt to set off a chain reaction of gobbling from other toms in the vicinity. But if you don't get a response, that's okay, too. At least you've narrowed the big country a bit and ruled out one potential roost. Travel a mile or more over to another canyon or oak grove the next morning. You can bet you'll hear toms gobbling there.

WESTERN TURKEY PROFILES

The Merriam's wild turkey, *Meleagris gallopavo merriami,* inhabits 15 western states, from South Dakota to Idaho to New Mexico. The birds gobble and strut in a variety of habitats, from plains to scrub-oak foothills to high mountains thick with ponderosa pines.

A Merriam's gobbler is about the same size as an Eastern tom. The dry, rocky terrain often sands down the tips of the westerner's spurs, and to a lesser degree his scraggly beard, giving the gobbler a lot of character. A tom's tail coverts and fan tips—long, silky and white—are distinctive. To many observers, the Merriam's is the most striking of the four subspecies of American turkeys.

The Rio Grande subspecies (above) falls somewhere between the Eastern and the Merriam's in range and appearance, hence its scientific classification, *Meleagris gallopavo intermedia.* Although the Rio lives in 13 central and western states, you might call it the "Texas turkey." Approximately 85 percent of America's Rio Grande population lives in the Lone Star State.

The Rio is a stocky bird. A mature gobbler has long, pink legs and weighs 18 to 24 pounds. His feathers show a coppery sheen in the plains sunlight. Like the Merriam's, a Rio Grande tom often has rubbed spurs, though his beard is typically longer and thicker.

Rule the Roost

with Ron Jolly

These days it's tougher than ever to trick an old gobbler first thing in the morning. Why? Because many toms roost with two, three or more hens throughout the spring courting season. A longbeard might sit on his limb and bellow at your clucks and yelps, but why should he fly down and walk your way? The old boy has what he wants at his beck and call. When his hens fly from their trees at daybreak, the tom pitches out to them. The turkeys mill around and breed awhile, and then drift off to a feeding or strutting area. You're left to sit and call and wonder what the heck went wrong.

So what should you do, sleep in and never hunt early again? Hardly. Playing cat and mouse with a tom at sunrise remains the essence of the spring game.

"First thing in the morning, I like for a turkey to gobble on his own, and I give him time to do it," says Ron Jolly. "Instead of pulling out a locator call and blasting away like a lot of people do, I keep still and listen. Most of the time a crow will fly over and caw, or an owl or coyote will light up. If a turkey is roosted close by, he'll usually gobble at that."

The Alabama pro knows that sometimes you have to force the action. "If it's getting close to fly-down time and I haven't heard a turkey, I'll give a one-note hoot with my voice, or blow a crow call," says Jolly. "If I still don't hear a gobble, I go someplace else."

The Expert: **Ron Jolly** of Tuskegee, Alabama, shot his first gobbler when he was 12 years old. Thirty-eight years later he is still going strong, hunting and now filming wild turkeys for a living. Jolly, one of the nation's top outdoor videographers, is executive producer of the *Outdoor Alabama* television show. Every March and April a good portion of his job is to call in and capture on film exciting hunts for Alabama's notoriously tough toms. Here's how Jolly rules the roost each morning.

When you go out in the
evening to roost a tom
for the next morning's
hunt, listen not only for
gobbles, but also for
other turkey sounds.
You might hear birds
shuffling leaves as they
move into a roost site,
or you might hear a
hen clucking and
yelping. Listen for the
wing beats of turkeys
flying up for the night
(you can hear the
ruckus for 150 yards
or more when the wind
is still). If one heavy
bird thumps up, you've
probably located a
solo tom. If you hear
multiple turkeys stagger
up into trees, you'll have
to deal with sassy hens
in the morning. Either
way, you need to know
so you can tailor your
calling to the task at
hand.

◆◆◆◆◆◆◆◆

Zeroing in on a Bird

Listen for gobbler thunder from a hillside, ridge point or similar vantage each morning. The higher you hunt, the easier it is to hear and course gobbles.

"My daddy taught me a long time ago that the secret to hearing is how you listen," says Jolly. "When I'm hunting with another person, I don't talk once we get into the woods. I walk off a little ways and stand alone in a spot where I can hear well in all directions."

When a gobbler roars, you'll jump. But don't take off down through the woods after him. "Listen and try to course the turkey," says Jolly. "It sounds weird, but I look down through the dark woods and try to visualize the exact tree and the exact limb a gobbler is on."

If a tom is roosted nearby, Jolly moves quickly toward him. "But if he's off in the distance, I move 50 yards or so in his direction, check up and wait for him to gobble again. I might stop another three or four times to get a solid line on the bird."

Keep in mind that when a tom gobbles facing you, he may sound closer than he really is. Conversely, a turkey that spins on his limb and roars in the opposite direction sounds farther away. The lay of the land and the thickness of the foliage can also make it difficult to judge the distance to a roosted bird. Just keep sneaking along and pinpointing gobbles.

Using terrain breaks and foliage for cover, you should have little trouble sneaking within 200 yards of a roosted turkey. "A lot of people talk about getting within 100 yards, but I tend to play it safe and set up 125 to 150 yards away, especially when I'm toting camera gear," notes Jolly. "I sure don't want a turkey to see or hear me setting up."

The bottom line: Sneak as close as you dare. The less ground between you and a tom, the better the odds he'll pitch down from the roost and come to your calls. But remember, this is also when you have the greater risk of bumping him.

Solid Setups

For some strange reason, toms are reluctant to move downhill to calling. Why? Hunters have been scratching their heads over this question for decades, but to this day, nobody knows for sure. Whatever the reason, always try to position above a roosted bird, or at least on the same gradient plane with him.

As you slip toward a gobbler, scan the misty woods for a fence, creek, gully or the like, and maneuver to take the hazard out of play. Try to set up where the terrain is gently rolling and fairly open, which makes it easy for a tom to fly down and strut to your calls.

Jolly adds a caveat, and it's a good one. "I try to set up where it's flat and open, but sometimes I intentionally put a log pile or maybe a thicket between a turkey and me," he says. "That way, when a gobbler flies down, he can't look 100 yards through the open woods to where I'm calling and see no hen. The turkey has to come in to 50 or 60 yards and walk around the obstacle to find the hen, so there's less chance he'll hang up. When he turns the corner, he's just about in range."

A good strategy is to anticipate where a gobbler will go to gather hens, then set up to block his way. Is there a field, clear-cut, oak flat or open creek bottom within a half-mile or so of a tom's roost tree? If so, circle around and set up on that side of a gobbling turkey. If the tom flies down and heads for his strut zone, you'll be in good position to cut him off and coax him the final few yards with calling.

Fly-Down Sounds

Set up and listen to a turkey's raucous gobbling, for it is one of the true wonders of nature. But don't become so enthralled that you miss other key sounds.

Listen for turkeys flying down from their roosts at dawn. Once the gobblers hit the ground, crank up your hen calling.

"Listen for clucking and yelping," says Jolly, "and pinpoint the location of any hens in the area. Let's say you hear hens roosted 100 yards to the west of a gobbler. If the gobbler flies down and shuts up, where do you think he went? Well, west for sure. If you have to move on him, go that way."

Also take note of other toms that gobble off in the distance. If your first hunt is a bust, you'll need to go to one of those other turkeys.

At daybreak, listen for turkeys swishing and crashing to the forest floor. Those wing beats tell you a lot. Did just one big turkey thump down? If so, your target gobbler is alone, and you have no immediate competition from hens. But if you hear several birds stagger from their limbs, you can bet hens were roosted nearby. You'll need to crank up your calling, and we'll get to that later.

On the bright side, a heavy flurry of wings might indicate that a subordinate or "fringe" tom was roosted alongside the gobbling bird. Be ready for a silent strutter to come to your calls.

Most toms pitch straight down from trees at daybreak, then strut around and gobble awhile. But on occasion, a gobbler will sail away from you. This probably means one of two things: The tom feels more comfortable traveling that way, or hens might be dragging him in the opposite direction. Either way, it's probably best to get up and go. Try to circle around and re-position in front of him. Float soft, seductive calls from your new setup, and you might fool the tom yet.

Once in a blue moon a tom will fly off his limb toward you. This is obviously what you want, so don't blow it. Tune in to the wing beats, and the instant the bird crash-lands, ease your body and shotgun in his direction. The turkey will not see you move as he gathers himself after the short flight. You'll be positioned nicely for the bird's final approach to your calls.

Calling Tips

It's the dream scenario. You slip within 100 yards of a turkey that's roosted alone and gobbling hot and heavy. The more the bird roars, the more you get this uncontrollable urge to cluck and yelp. Fight it! Too much calling can hang a tom on his limb as he waits for the "hen" (you) to sail or walk beneath his roost tree. The longer he sits up there and fails to see a girl, the more likely it is that he'll smell a rat. When the bird finally flies down 15 or 20 minutes later, there's a good chance he'll go the other way.

Lots of loud, fancy calling has another downside: It's apt to keep a roosted tom gobbling his head off. That is thrilling to hear, but it is not something you want. There's a huge risk that the turkey will gobble up hens or, worse, another hunter in the area. Either way, your hunt is probably ruined.

"If I know a turkey is by himself, with no hens anywhere around, I always wait for him to fly down before I make my first call," says Jolly. "That's a tough thing to do, but it's the right thing to do."

When a bachelor's feet hit the dirt, Jolly goes to work. He takes the turkey's temperature and tailors his calls accordingly. "If a turkey is hot and gobbling hard, a few clucks and yelps might be all it takes," he says. "But some birds are not so hot and need more calling." In this case, the Alabama pro cackles on a mouth call like a hen flying down, and he sometimes flaps an old hen wing for extra realism.

If a tom bellows at your first calls, whether they were soft or aggressive, shut the heck up for a while! He has honored you as a hen, he likes what he hears and he knows where you are. Let the turkey come look for you. If after a few minutes the tom fails to show, cluck and yelp to refocus his attention your way.

One morning a few years ago I slipped to within 120 yards of a turkey ripping it in an oak tree. That bird must have gobbled 100 times! His tree talk had a domino effect. Another tom began gobbling down the ridge, then another and another. Hens started yelping and

clucking. Pretty soon a dozen birds were raising the roof on the place.

I had two choices: to sit there like a wallflower, or jump right in. I chose the latter and started yelping and cutting on a diaphragm call. A couple of hens took great offense at me and called back aggressively. I mimicked their sassy yelps. The toms thundered harder.

It was barely shooting light when I heard a heavy bird thump down. In a surreal scene that I remember to this day, a huge gobbler with a shimmering white head strutted in beneath eight hens. The girls peered down from their limbs and called wildly as if to say, "Hey, big boy, what about us?" I nailed the longbeard, the hens scattered and the remaining toms gobbled at the gunshot.

While it's good to know how to handle those dream scenarios, the rules change when you run across a gobbler roosted with hens. In this situation, you ought to call while the turkeys are still on the roost. How else can you get into the game?

"When a gobbler has hens, I want him to answer me at least once," says Jolly. "I do whatever it takes to make that happen. If I cluck and the turkey gobbles, I might not call again. But if I have to scale up to loud yelps or a cackle to make him gobble, I do it. I want that gobbler to acknowledge me. I want him to think, 'There's one more hen over there I might need to check out.'"

Many mornings, whether he has hens or not, a gobbler just won't commit your way. How long should you fool with him?

"As long as I can keep contact with a gobbler, I'll sit for an hour or longer," says Jolly. "You never know when he'll break and come your way. But when I lose contact with a turkey, when he starts to drift out of calling range, I get up and go."

Sometimes the Alabama pro flanks a gobbler and calls to him from a different spot. Other times he leaves an ornery turkey and goes looking for a new bird to hunt. "There are no rules in turkey hunting," adds Jolly with a laugh. "Just do what feels right each morning."

LATE-SHIFT TOMS

ry as you might, most mornings you won't get a turkey right off the roost. Don't get down about it—get fired up for the fun that follows! Go back to your vehicle, take a break and have a second cup of joe during the gobbling lull that often occurs between 7 and 9 a.m., when toms and hens mate. Then, as the sun angles higher into the sky, get after them again.

Hike out a logging road or trail, stop on a ridge, and listen. You might hear a tom crank up his gobbling again, since his hens just left him to lay eggs or sit on their nests. If the boys are being tight-lipped, try to yank a gobble out of them. Blow a crow call or maybe a shrill hawk whistle. Hit the call hard. Passive clucking and yelping won't cut it from 9 a.m. till noon. You need more shocking power. "A box call works best for me in the middle of the day," says Ron Jolly. "I stroke loud, sharp yelps and cutts to make turkeys gobble."

Usually, you can expect fast action during the late shift. If you cover enough ground and call with zest, you'll strike your share of lovesick toms. Some of them, especially those hot two-year-olds, will gobble a time or two and come in fast. Be ready for that.

One morning a few years back, I cutt on a box call. A turkey triple-gobbled 200 yards away. I slipped forward, planning to cut the distance in half before setting up. Suddenly there was a flash of black, and the bird came running in, his body rocking and his thick beard swinging! I knelt in the brush and raised my shotgun. Somehow the tom didn't see me. I fired and checked my watch. I struck the turkey at 9:49 and shot him at 9:55.

As you "run and gun," wear camouflage gloves and a facemask around your neck. When a turkey bellows close, find a set-up tree fast. Pull up your mask, pull out your calls and point your shotgun out front. Don't fool around and spook a tom that might be churning in to your calls.

When a turkey gobbles at your calls from 250 or more yards away, things generally unfold in a more orderly manner. Walk toward the bird and blow a crow call. Hopefully the tom will shock-gobble a couple more times so you can get a good line on him. You might have to give him another hard yelp or cutt to make him roar. If he won't talk and you have lots of ground left to cover, forget him and move on. Using terrain wrinkles and foliage for cover, you should be able to sneak within 125 yards of the turkey. Still, beware those runners. If a turkey revs up his gobbling and starts closing the gap, sit down and get ready—he's coming!

Let's say you strike a tom that gobbles for an hour or so but fails to come in. Then he shuts up. There's only an hour left before quitting time at noon or 1 p.m. What do you do? I say sit tight and keep calling every 10 minutes until it's time to leave the woods. You never know what might happen.

One April a buddy and I raised a tom at 11:30 a.m. We worked the bird for an hour, until he finally shut up and drifted off. We had only 30 minutes left to hunt, so we decided, "What the heck, let's burn up the woods with calling!"

We yelped, cutt and threw in some fighting purrs and gobbles. Pretty soon a different turkey gobbled. We swiveled around our set-up trees and spotted not one but two longbeards strutting in across a pasture. The dominant bird gobbled 10 times as he and his submissive brother honed in on our calls. My friend and I doubled at 15 yards! I checked my watch: 12:50 p.m. We slung the three-year-old toms over our shoulders and hiked out of the woods with 10 minutes of hunting time to spare.

Here's one last tactic, and it's a good one. Stay in the woods late a couple of mornings in a row. Look and listen for hens and gobblers, but don't pressure the birds with fancy calling. Just try to pattern where they go to feed and strut in the middle of the day. A long oak ridge or bench, a wide, open creek bottom, or a green field would be good terrain to check out.

"If you hunt the same places all season, it's pretty easy to figure out where turkeys hang out in the middle of the day," says Jolly. "I've got this saying. If a turkey does it two days in a row, you never know. If he does it three days in a row, you ought to be able to kill him."

If Jolly sees or hears a gobbler on a flat or in a field at 10 a.m. two days running, he sets up there the third day around 9 a.m. and waits for the old boy to show. Sometimes he doesn't even have to call. "I've shot a lot of old turkeys that way," says the Alabama pro, with a satisfied grin.

Fall Turkey Tactics

with Jim Clay

I n the spring a tom turkey is a
playboy that struts and gobbles
and treads as many hens as he can.
But by May's end he sheds that skin,
and come October he is an aloof,
shut-mouthed bachelor once again. An
old bird hooks up with a few long-
bearded cronies and off they go. The
vagabonds can be tough to find and
even tougher to call if you can pin 'em
down. Are you up to the challenge?

Find the Flocks

You can't miss the sign of a mixed
flock of turkeys feeding through the
autumn woods. Such a flock, usually
made up of 10 to 20 hens, jakes and
jennies, tills up wide swaths of leaves
and duff as the birds search for mast,
bugs, green shoots and other food-
stuffs. Ah, but a ton of sign is not
what you're looking for.

"If you find lots of scratchings on a
ridge or in a creek bottom, go somewhere else to look for gobblers," says
Clay. "Old toms will hang in the same
area with hens and young turkeys if
there's just one good food source—say,
acorns—on the ground. But most of
the time the gobblers stay off to them-
selves." If it's windy, check for turkeys
loafing in hollows and other low
spots.

Look for pockets of large, deep
scratchings, especially at the base of
trees and fallen logs. "Toms kick back
leaves and lay big wakes as they
scratch, whereas hens often just pick

The Expert: When it comes to hunting and calling
wild turkeys in autumn, **Jim Clay** of Winchester,
Virginia, is one of the best. For more than 40 years
Clay has roamed the hills and hollows of the Old
Dominion, where the pursuit of turkeys from
October through December is more ritual than
sport. Clay owned and operated Perfection Turkey
Calls until his retirement a few years ago. Now he
spends his time bass fishing, hunting whitetails
and, yes, calling for long-bearded gobblers every
day during the spring and fall seasons.

• A 12-gauge pump or autoloader choked full or super-full is the ticket. When shooting at toms through thick foliage in the spring, you might use three-inch loads of No. 4 or 5 shot. But try No. 6 shot, which throws a larger pattern, when hunting in open fall woods. Be sure to test various choke/load combinations when switching firepower from spring to fall. No. 4s and No. 6s will probably pattern a little differently in your shotgun.

• Wear a camouflage pattern heavy with browns and grays to match the fall or winter woods. If gun season for deer is also open, wear an orange cap or vest when walking the woods.

◆◆◆◆◆◆◆

and stir in the leaves," notes Clay. "Those wakes of leaves point in the direction the gobblers fed, so it's pretty easy to follow them."

Scout for gobbler tracks (the middle toes are 2½ to 3½ inches long) and droppings (large, J-shaped hooks splashed with white) in old roadbeds and along field edges and creeks. And look for feathers. "Turkeys go through a couple of autumn molts," says Clay. "Check for the black breast feathers of gobblers in feeding areas and beneath roost trees."

Be an Early Bird

"Spring or fall, turkeys are most vocal at daybreak," Clay explains. "In fact, in October and November flocks talk more the first hour than they do the rest of the day combined. But for some strange reason, many fall hunters don't get into the woods early. It's just like the spring. If you

miss the first hour, you've missed the best time to hear turkeys."

So get out there at first light and head for a likely roost. Pines that border a creek or an oak ridge near a crop field are a good bet. Stop and listen as pink strokes the sky. Hear a bunch of yelping, cackling and aggravated purring? Well, that is the jam session of a mixed flock, so you'd better go elsewhere for old toms.

Slip out another ridge, perk up your ears and listen for an odd sound: a deep cluck or a two- or three-note "croaking yelp." Those two vocalizations make up 90 percent of gobbler talk in the fall. Sometimes a tom will short-gobble on a fall morning, but don't count on it. Listen for a cluck or a croak, along with the wing beats of four to six birds flying down for the day. "Depending on the terrain, you can hear calls and wings up to 200 yards away on a calm morning," says Clay.

Look for the black-tipped chest feathers of toms near feeding and roosting sites.

In the fall, scout for a flock of longbeards feeding in a pasture or crop field. Whe you find the birds, use gobbler clucks and yelps to call them in.

Your best chance at a longbeard is right off the roost. If you hear a cluck or yelp, slip close—within 100 yards of the birds if terrain and cover allow. "Try to set up between the gobblers and a feeding area, maybe a cornfield or an oak ridge with scratching," suggests Clay. "That's where they'll go." Do a little calling. A flock might not come in, but a couple of toms might break off and come for a peek.

The key here is "a little calling." If you hammer toms with lusty yelps or cutts like you do in the spring, you're apt to shut them up and drive them away. In fact, any hen call might send the boys packing. Remember, toms batch it now. About all they'll respond to is the lonesome call of a pal looking for male companionship.

The first call to make is a deep gobbler cluck. Follow it up with a slow, croaking yelp. Sometimes I toss in a half-gobble to see if an old turkey will gobble back and give away his location—a long shot. Call sparingly for an hour or so, and watch for longbeards that might never appear.

The truth is, most mornings you won't see or hear any turkeys. No problem. Hang tough in the woods. Keep walking ridges and listen. "Each flock of turkeys is different once it hits the ground in the morning," notes Clay. "I've seen toms fly down and take off running. Other birds leave their trees and start to feed. Most of the time turkeys will pitch down, preen, mill around, scratch and do a little calling. Cover some ground and listen for turkey sounds that first hour. You might find a flock yet."

A Midmorning Stroll

When the sun comes up, gobblers go to brunch. Early in the season, and especially during a lean mast year, you might spot them nabbing grasshoppers or pecking grain in fields. But most days the bachelors hang in the woods and roam widely in search of wild grapes, beechnuts, dogwood berries and especially acorns. Lay down the boot leather, look for fresh scratchings, follow the wakes and try to intercept a gang.

Hike high, but don't skyline. Walk beneath the crests of ridges and hills and glass for flocks in draws and creek bottoms. Pause often and listen for turkeys calling or raking in the leaves. Oh yeah, I almost forgot. Make sure you do the "turkey walk."

When it's hot and dry in the fall, game can hear you coming in the leaves for hundreds of yards. "If deer don't smell you, they'll sometimes get curious, stop and look back to see what's up," says Clay. "But turkeys don't do that. When they hear something big and mean coming, they get the heck out of there. Several times I've heard birds running in the leaves. I stopped and watched flocks zoom past. Fifteen minutes later hunters strolled by without knowing they'd spooked 'em!"

So it pays to walk like a turkey. "Step, step, scratch leaves with your boots, step, step and scratch again," says Clay. "You can sometimes walk right up on a flock of turkeys like that. Sounds strange, but try it."

As you prospect around the woods, float a gobbler cluck or yelp every once in a while. You never know, a bird might answer and tip off his location. Suppose a gobbler clucks back, or you spot a flock in a draw or creek bottom below? You have two options.

First, you can set up above the birds and do a little calling. One November afternoon Clay got lucky and spotted a couple of longbeards in a bottom. He sneaked around and up to a bluff, set up and clucked and yelped for two hours. "I was about to give up when I heard leaves crunching behind me," he recalls. "I swiveled around in the nick of time and nailed a third big turkey coming over the ridge."

Strange things can happen in the autumn woods. You never know when or where you might bump into a longbeard. "Maybe another hunter, or a coyote or fox, spooked him away from his buddies, or perhaps he just wandered off for a while," says Clay. "Keep your eyes and ears open for a straggler. He might fall for your calls."

Option number two is the much-ballyhooed bust, which is easier said than done. Let's say you spot five gobblers down in a creek bottom. Use terrain and cover to sneak close to the flock from above. Lay down your 12-gauge or bow and sprint toward

FALL GOBBLER TALK		
Call	**Description**	**How to Make It**
Gobbler Cluck	Most frequent fall call; deep and coarse; sounds like "pock" or "yawk"	Pop the lid of a raspy box; pop a wooden striker in the deep-pitched center of a slate or glass call
Gobbler Yelp	2- or 3-note sequence; deep, croaking pitch; sounds like "yawk, yawk, yawk"; slower in cadence than hen yelp	Croak slowly on a multi-reed diaphragm; stroke 2 or 3 slow notes on a box; work a wooden peg slowly in the middle of a slate or glass call
Gobble	Less intense and fainter in fall than in spring; often a short "half gobble"	Try short, fluttering bursts of air on a tube call; shake a rubber gobble hose lightly

the birds, yelling like a wild man or barking like a dog. It sounds weird, but it can work. If you can split one or two longbeards from their mates, you have a fighting chance to call 'em back.

Walk a couple hundred yards in the direction the toms flew. Again, set up high on a ridge or point, where birds feel most comfortable coming to calls. Wait an hour or so for the woods to calm down, and then float a cluck or yelp. Maybe toss in a faint gobble. A lost tom might come back, or he might not. "Some old birds are content to roost and feed alone for days or weeks," notes Clay. "Heck, they might batch it all winter."

Last Call

Even outside Mexico, turkeys take a siesta from around noon till 2:00 p.m. "I think it's the hardest time to find flocks," says Clay. "The birds seem to go into a loafing mode and don't move much. All you can do is keep walking and calling." In hot, dry weather, look for toms feeding along creeks and around secluded ponds and springs.

Along about 2:30, things pick up. Flocks begin moving and scratching again. Check for turkeys in feeding areas you've yet to hit, or circle back and check mast thickets or oak ridges and bottoms you might have hunted earlier that day.

"If I find fresh scratchings on a ridge or flat with lots of food, especially acorns, I stop and hunt there the rest of the day," says Clay. "But I tone down my calling as the afternoon progresses. I cluck and yelp so that turkeys up to 200 yards away can hear me. A flock might think other turkeys are feeding over there and come in. Even if I don't shoot a bird, there's a good chance the turkeys will roost close by. If I hear or see 'em flying up into trees, I know where to hunt first thing the next morning. You can't beat that."

TURKEY DOGS

They run far and wide, scent-trailing flocks and then barreling headlong into the birds, yipping and barking to scatter hens and toms to high heaven. "Turkey dogs" inject rowdiness into the otherwise serene fall game.

Renegade pointers, setters and "droppers" (pointer/setter crosses) are the most common and popular turkey dogs. Some breeders cross setters with hounds to create dogs with even stronger scent-trailing and barking traits.

It's pretty obvious why a turkey dog must have a full-choke nose and, given the wheels of a 20-pound gobbler, a strong set of legs and lungs. But why must he bark like mad? Easy. The dog yaps to let its master know when and where it just busted a flock. The hunter then hustles over to the bust site, builds a little blind, settles in with his canine friend (his work done, the dog generally snoozes) and calls back the birds.

Some 15 states permit dogs for fall turkey hunting (nowhere are dogs legal during the spring season). By far the hotbeds of the sport are Virginia, West Virginia and New York. Where legal, try training that hardheaded, big-running bird dog of yours to trail, locate and scatter turkeys. The best way to do it is to hook up with a seasoned turkey dog man. Run your raw recruit with his dog, until yours gets the hang of the game.

HUNTING THE FOUR SUBSPECIES OF TURKEYS

Team Turkey Hunting

with Chuck Jones

he NBA has the Lakers. The Yankees might be baseball's best squad ever. But hey, sports junkies, don't you know that turkey hunting has a dream team of its own? For more than ten years, Chuck Jones and world-class caller Walter Parrott have bonded like brothers in the woods. Traveling across North America, the duo has called in and shot a staggering number of long-beards—on film, no less! Their winning tactics will help you and a buddy score more beards and spurs.

Know Your Teammate

Deer hunting is best when you go it alone. But turkey hunting is a great time for camaraderie. "No doubt, a pair of turkey hunters can have a lot of fun, not to mention trick a lot of toms," says Jones.

Jones and Parrott have been hunting together for so long now that they've developed an uncanny ability to understand each other in the woods. "No matter what the situation, I pretty much know what Walter is thinking," says Jones. "I can predict his next move, whether it's moving on a gobbler, sitting tight, calling, whatever."

Jones notes that it takes time—at least a couple of seasons—to forge a bond like that. But getting the knack of reading your partner is important. "You need to get on the same wavelength and think alike. It makes your hunts smoother and more productive."

The Expert: **Chuck Jones** of Cadiz, Kentucky, is one of the best pure turkey hunters in the country. But these days Jones rarely hunts alone. As cameraman and producer of Knight & Hale's videos and television show, Jones spends his spring mornings set up behind a caller (or two), trying to film another successful turkey hunt. The job has made Jones somewhat of a clairvoyant. The guy has a knack for reading his partners' minds and anticipating their every move—just what it takes to tag-team a tom.

QUICK
TIP

◆◆◆◆◆◆◆◆

Two hunters are plenty, but if a third buddy wants to tag along one morning, let him. Be safe and carry unloaded shotguns until you set up on a gobbler. Then, two hunters should sit together beside a tree and load up. The third person in your party (the best caller) should sit 20 to 40 yards behind the shooters. He never loads his gun. His job is to yelp and, hopefully, pull a turkey within range of his pals.

◆◆◆◆◆◆◆◆

Jones believes that good chemistry is a big key to a team's success. "You and your partner should have the same basic views on hunting. Otherwise, you'll be going in one direction while your buddy is thinking and doing the opposite," he says.

In other words, if you are a patient hunter who likes to move slowly through the woods and sit and call in one spot for up to an hour, find a buddy who likes that style, too. If you're a mover and shaker who covers a lot of ground and calls aggressively, hunt with a pal who also likes to "cutt and run." Seeing eye to eye will help you slip around the woods, go to a turkey and set up to call. In turn, you'll shoot more gobblers.

Respect Each Other

I've had the pleasure of sharing the woods with Jones and Parrott, and the thing that struck me was that these guys genuinely like each other. Sure, they're friendly and quick with a laugh or a jab, but more important, you can see and feel how they trust and respect each other. Those are the cornerstones of the team's success.

"Walter is a good, safe hunter who has a ton of woods savvy and turkey wisdom," says Jones. "And of course the way he yelps—he's probably the best turkey caller in the world—makes it pretty easy for me. I trust what he says and does, and vice versa. That gives us confidence—something every hunting team needs."

One spring Jones and Parrott hunted a public area in New York. There were camouflaged hunters running around and yelping everywhere. Parrott has long hunted public ground in his home state of Missouri, so the pressure didn't faze him much. But Jones grew up hunting a lot of private leases in the Deep South. All those other hunters bummed him out.

One evening the hunters were out roosting when, just before dark, a big gobbler ran across a gravel road, his beard swinging. "I knew that turkey would roost nearby, but since he was so close to the road, I also figured three or four other hunters would be on him the next morning," says Jones. "But Walter said, 'What the heck, let's go in there and try him.'" Jones moaned some, but then he relented.

The next morning Parrott hooted and the turkey gobbled up on a ridge. The hunters circled around, set up and called in the bird just like that. "He had a great beard and sharp spurs, and you know what, we didn't see or hear another hunter all morning," Jones says with a laugh. "Man, I'm glad I trusted my buddy on that one."

Jones' faith in his partner made that hunt. "I had confidence in my friend's wisdom and calling, and I handed him the reins. It paid off with a big turkey on video." Jones has returned the favor and picked up Parrott many times, too.

Two-Way Communication

Over time, a pair of hunters develop an open line of communication that is vital to tricking toms. "Whether we're slipping toward a gobbling turkey or setting up, Walter and I take our time and talk things over," says Jones. "We don't waste a lot of time doing it, but we want to make sure we're on the same track as a hunt unfolds."

Differences of opinions and moments of confusion still can, and do, crop up. So before you head out each morning determine who will be in charge of the day's hunt. "Like the old saying goes, two chiefs is one too many," mentions Jones. "Walter and I hunt a lot alike, and we talk over things, like how far away a turkey is, where to set up and how much to call. But it still makes sense for one of us to call the final shots when a hunt really heats up. There's no confusion that way."

No hunter is on top of his or her game all the time. One day your partner's mindset might be a

TWO-MAN TACTICS

Here are a few suggestions to make team hunting more enjoyable:

• Early in the morning it can pay for you and a buddy to split up. Two pairs of ears listening in opposite directions can pick up the faint gobbles of birds roosted in bottoms or on distant hillsides. Meet back up with your partner 10 minutes before sunrise and compare notes.

• Later in the morning, strike off along a ridge together. Before you call, put at least 25 yards between you. As one of you yelps the other keeps still and listens closely. Often the listener will hear a gobble that the caller can't.

• Unless you're shooting a video like Jones and Parrott, you and your pal should usually set up and work a gobbler side by side, against the same big tree. How far is the turkey? Did he just gobble again? Can you see him? Should we move? It's a snap to whisper and communicate.

• Say a turkey gobbles for 30 minutes, but hangs up 100 yards away. Have your partner sit tight while you sneak back 20, 30 or 50 yards. Cutt, yelp and scratch leaves as you go. Thinking the hen is tiring of the game and moving off, an ornery tom might break strut and follow. The old boy might walk right into your buddy's lap.

• When a gobbler struts 100 yards or more away, give him a concert of calling (within reason, of course). Maybe you cluck and purr on a slate while your friend yelps and cutts on a mouth call or box. If a turkey gobbles well at the mouth call and moves toward it, you should shut up and let your pal work the bird. Continue to read the gobbling and moves of the tom. If he likes "rock-and-roll" calling, hammer away, again within reason. But if a tom hangs up and shies from aggressive calls, tone them down.

• On a day when turkeys won't gobble, try this trick: You cutt on a box or an aluminum call. Your buddy stands 25 yards away and follows it up with a booming gobble on a tube or rubber shaker. Sometimes a burst of breeding calls will make a tight-lipped strutter roar.

little off, and that in turn disrupts the routine. The next day your buddy might be sharper and more "gobbler-ready" than you are. Talk it over, and decide who's the best person for the day's job.

Talking is one thing. But you know you and your buddy have arrived as a team when you get the non-verbal communication down pat. Jones and Parrott have learned to read each other's body language. "I can look at Walter walking through the woods and tell when and where he's going to stop and call," says Jones. "He doesn't have to say anything, which saves time and might even keep us from spooking a turkey that is close. I immediately stop 50 to 60 yards away and listen as he calls. Walter knows I'm doing that, listening in one direction, so he naturally listens the other way. If a turkey gobbles, one of us will hear him."

How two guys slip in and set up on a gobbler will make or break the hunt. "I watch Walter sneaking along in front of me, and I can usually guess which tree he's gonna pick for a setup," says Jones. "He might glance back at me, but he doesn't have to say anything. He knows that once he sets up, I'll position the camera in a good spot close behind him."

Sometimes as a turkey gobbles and works in, the hunters communicate with little hand signals. For example, Jones might pinch his fingers together to tell Parrott to yelp again. Parrott might give the "slash across the throat" signal to say nope, I'm not calling any more. But mostly they just read each other's body language.

"If Walter moves his head or shotgun an inch, I know he sees a gobbler, or maybe he hears a bird drumming or walking in the leaves," says Jones. "I just point my camera that way and get ready."

Most of the time a gobbler will show up soon, tail fanned and white head gleaming. Parrott will shoot, and Jones will capture the action on film. The hunters walk out and admire their flopping prize before shooting the closing segment of the video. They smile and shake hands or high-five. "It's pretty special," Jones says with a smile.

Have Fun

One intangible is largely responsible for the amazing success of the Knight & Hale dream team. "We're in the woods filming for a living, trying to make good TV and videos," says Jones. "Walter and I are serious about what we do, but we try not to lose sight of what's really important—having fun. And you know what? The more fun we have, the more turkeys we usually get."

TURNING TWO

Say you and a buddy are sitting side by side with a couple of longbeards roaring and coming to your calls. Here's how to "turn two" and drop both birds with a couple of well-placed shots.

Split the area in front of your set-up tree smack down the middle. You cover the right side while your buddy watches left, or vice versa. As the toms gobble, drum and approach, scan the foliage on your flank for open shooting lanes. Both hunters should have their shotguns up on their knees and pointed safely out front.

At this juncture don't try to decide who will fire first. Hang loose and flow with the turkeys. How and where the toms come in will dictate the shooting scenario.

The instant you lay eyes on one or both of the gobblers, whisper to your partner. He should do the same. Keep whispering and tracking the birds as they approach.

Sometimes a couple of longbeards will strut in 10 to 30 yards apart; one bird might be 5 to 20 steps in front of the other one. Ah, this is tough! One hunter should ease his shotgun barrel into position, cover the lead gobbler and let him keep coming. Hopefully the second tom will drift into range before the first bird spooks (either he makes one of you out, or more likely, he gets nervous because he doesn't see a hen in the area). But if the lead gobbler putts, turns and begins to walk away, whoever is on him should shoot right then. One gobbler on the ground is better than two running off in the bush.

The dream scenario—something that comes along maybe once every few seasons—is for a pair of longbeards to strut in wing to wing. Don't blow it! With the birds at 40 yards and closing, determine your targets. Whisper to your buddy something like, "You take the turkey on the right, I'll shoot the left one." Get your gun barrels on the right birds and keep them there.

Now finalize the shooting order. For starters, forget about the "1-2-3-fire" thing. I've learned the hard way that if two hunters try to fire their shotguns simultaneously, one or both shooters are bound to get nervous and jump the gun or flinch. You might miss one or—yikes!—both toms.

One member of the team, generally the less experienced hunter, should plan to shoot first. The second hunter must have the ability to remain cool and make the quick shot he is bound to get.

Okay, here goes. Let the toms strut inside 30 yards. Keep whispering to each other, making sure you both can see the birds and shoot through openings in the foliage. Then the first shooter takes a deep breath, flicks off his safety and says, "I'm gonna take him." He fires and sits tight.

The second hunter has, oh, about a nanosecond to react. At the shot, the second gobbler will stick up his white-crowned head for an instant before running or flying away. Shooter number two must cover those reddish-blue wattles and fire quicker than you can say, "We just doubled!"

With the pressure off, the fun begins. Trot out to the flopping turkeys. High-five and slap your buddy's back. Check out those two awesome beards and those four sharp spurs. Savor the moment. In turkey hunting, it doesn't get any better than that.

Make a Shooting Plan

with Michael Waddell

Most hunters approach a gobbling turkey and set up where they think they might call in the bird. Michael Waddell sneaks in and plops down where he knows he can shoot a tom if it walks in. "I don't always look for the biggest tree or even the prettiest calling spot," says the Georgia pro. "I'm more concerned with setting up where I have at least one good shooting lane. I'm not afraid to sit beside a little tree or against some brush out in the open if that's where I can get the best shot at a turkey."

Sit down, get comfortable and get organized before you call to a tom roosted or gobbling on the ground 100 yards or so away. Raise your shotgun and swing it from side to side. Snap or trim any saplings, briars or brush that may snag the gun barrel (or the gun's sling) if you shift left or right to shoot.

Now get into the "turkey shooter's coil." Slump low against a tree, pull up your knees and level your shotgun across them. If you shoot right-handed, set up with your left shoulder pointed toward where a turkey gobbled and where you think he'll come in. "That way you can easily cover a bird if he walks in anywhere out front, and you can swing well if he comes in off to your left," notes Waddell. If you're a southpaw, sit with your right shoulder pointed toward where you think a tom will approach.

Move It!

Many turkeys strut in on a straight line. But others veer left or right. A few flank and circle as they come looking for the source of your calls. You never know, so keep a tom covered. Each time he rips a gobble out in the brush, ease your body and shotgun in his direction.

"When a turkey gobbles and starts coming in, a lot of hunters freeze up," says Waddell. "They're scared to death to move. Big mistake! When a bird is still a good ways out there, he can't see you move, so go for it. Get your body turned and your gun pointed in the right direction."

Put your instincts on red alert, and keep panning as the tom closes in. Listen for a turkey walking in the leaves, or spitting and drumming. You might hear the swish of a bird coming through a field or brush. A hen might purr in front of a gobbler. Flow with those sounds and ease into good shooting position.

Stay Calm

There he is! Take a deep breath to calm your nerves and still your racing heart. A long-bearded turkey waddles in, jerking his head and craning his neck, exploding into strut and gobbling so close you think he'll blow the camo cap off your head. A scene like that can cause even the most seasoned hunter to come unglued.

Chill and focus on the tom's head. When an old gobbler is fired up and coming for a hen, his noggin is big and white as a softball, but it might turn Carolina blue before your eyes. Know your target and then be doubly sure. Look for a long beard arcing like a hand sickle from a tom's black breast.

The Expert: **Michael Waddell** of Waverly Hall, Georgia, has been hunting wild turkeys for 15 years. As compared to the other experts in this book, Waddell is a "young gun," and in more ways than one. He is an ace cameraman and producer for Realtree Camouflage's TV show and videos. He's hot on the competitive turkey-calling circuit. Waddell is also one of the best in the business when it comes time to pull the trigger and close the deal with a tom.

Fine-Tune Your Position

Now it is almost crunch time—and still not the time to freeze up. "Keep your eye on the gobbler and react when you can," suggests Waddell. If a tom ducks his head behind a tree, log or pocket of brush, ease your shotgun to cover an opening where the tom will reappear. "Do it smoothly but quickly. Be ready to kill that turkey when he pops out on the other side of a tree or brush, before he gets to a bad spot where you might not be able to shoot."

Another good time to fine-tune your position is when a strutter turns away from you and hides his head behind his great fan. But you've got to move quickly. An old turkey is prone to drop strut and look around for danger, and he seems to have eyes in the back of his head. So don't fool around and move your gun too slowly.

Do everything right and a sharp-eyed tom will catch a flicker of movement every once in awhile. Most of the time it's no big deal. "When a gobbler comes in, he's not looking for a hunter," says Waddell, "he's looking for a hen. He expects to see her moving around. As long as you don't make any fast, crazy moves, the turkey shouldn't spook. Heck, he might stick up his head and give you a great shot."

Look for Pattern Busters

A lot of the time you'll have to shoot a turkey through leaves, grass or thin brush. "Don't worry—your shot will cut a path right through that," says Waddell. However, you must look for heavier stuff that can destroy a shot pattern. It's something hunters often fail to do in the heat of battle.

"It's easy to focus so hard on a turkey's head that you miss a big limb or a sapling between you and the bird," notes the Georgia pro. "If you shoot down a limb or tree, you're probably going to miss. Make sure

you have a clear shooting lane all the way out to the turkey, and don't over-look a tree five feet or so in front of your gun barrel. It's easy to look right past the close stuff."

Most of the time you can simply lean a few inches to a foot left or right to take a pattern-busting obstacle out of play.

How Close?

Most of us tote a 12-gauge autoloader or pump with a souped-up full or extra-full choke. We shoot 3- or 3½-inch magnum loads of No. 4, 5 or 6 shot (see the sidebar). There's no doubt we can drop toms out to 45 yards on occasion. But it takes a lot of luck to make those long shots.

At 40 yards and beyond, aligning a shotgun's front barrel bead on a turkey's head and neck vitals is pretty much a guessing game—the bead blots out most of the turkey. A scope on a turkey gun can help to alleviate this problem. Still, it is impossible to know how an expanding shot pattern will hold up as it clips brush, saplings and limbs out to 40 steps and beyond. Since long shots are so risky, it's usually best to hold your fire.

If a bird is calm and coming on a line to your calls, let him walk closer. "To me, 20 to 30 yards is perfect," says Waddell. "If you use one of today's tightly choked guns and a heavy load, and if you put a bead anywhere on a turkey's head and neck and don't pull the shot, you'll get him."

Is that tom 30 yards away…35…40? Some people have a devil of a time determining the range to a turkey, especially across an open field or plain. To keep from messing up and shooting at a bird that is too far away, there are a couple of things you can do. Before you begin calling, stake a decoy 30 yards from your set-up tree. Or sit down, pull a laser rangefinder from your vest and zap a big tree, rock or stump 30 yards away. When a gobbler struts inside your marker—decoy, stump, whatever—take him.

The 12-gauge shotgun is the ticket for the majority of America's turkey hunters. Women and kids can get by with a 20-gauge if they choose the right load and shoot at gobblers within 30 yards. If you are of the mindset that "bigger is better," and if you can handle a gun that kicks like a mule, you can go with a 10-gauge. But you don't really need it for turkey hunting.

Carry a three-shot repeater, either an autoloader or a pump. Rarely will you shoot at a tom three times—you will either miss him cleanly or drop him cleanly with your first shot or your second. But gobblers are tough, and sometimes a bird will surprise you by rolling up and trying to run or fly away. A third shot can be the difference between a trophy and a lost bird.

Remington, Benelli, Browning and Winchester manufacture quality autoloaders for turkey hunting. If you're a pump-gun shooter, more power to you. A shell-shucker fires just as fast as an autoloader and is less prone to jamming in the woods. Some of the aforementioned companies, along with Mossberg, offer good pumps for the game. All modern shotguns designed specifically for turkey hunting come with Realtree or Mossy Oak camouflage finishes.

The trend toward 21- to 24-inch, vent-rib barrels on turkey guns has been a grand innovation. Ballistics studies show that a shot charge fired through a short barrel does not lose significant velocity as compared to a load blown through a 26- or 28-inch tube. A short-barreled magnum offers an adequate sighting plane and wields easily around brush and saplings at your calling setups.

Gobblers are tough, and most of the time you're shooting at them through some foliage in the spring. For that, you need dense shot patterns, and all new turkey guns come with extra-full or super-full choke tubes. In addition, many companies manufacture aftermarket turkey tubes with even tighter constrictions. You ought to experiment with a variety of chokes and loads to see which throw the densest and most consistent patterns at 20, 30 and 40 yards.

The days of silver or white beads on a shotgun barrel are gone. Good riddance, because they were difficult to align on a gobbler's head and neck, especially early in the morning and when a bird was more than 30 yards away. Today, fiber-optic sights are the rage. The orange, green or yellow beads are easy to see and pin on a turkey in both low-light and bright-light conditions. Fiber-optic sights, front and rear, come standard on new turkey guns, or you can easily install them on your old magnum.

Some hunters mount low-power scopes on their magnums. The benefits: A crosshair is easy to pin on a gobbler's neck, and if your gun is sighted-in properly, your shot pattern will fly true every time. A drawback: A scope limits your field of view, which sometimes makes it tough to pick up an incoming tom. You might want to try a scope, especially if you're having trouble getting shot patterns to fly true, or if you missed more than one turkey last season. Several optics manufacturers market good scopes for turkey guns.

The "Big Three" turkey loads include Federal Premium, Remington Premier Magnum and Winchester Double X Magnum. Three-inch loads have always done a fine job for me, but some hunters use the heavier 3½-inch loads in new guns chambered for them. Also, check out the new high-velocity turkey loads from the ammo companies. They typically have ½-ounce less shot than standard magnum loads, but they produce 150 to 175 fps more velocity to reach out and touch toms.

You should also take a look at the new tungsten-nickel-iron loads offered by several ammo companies. These pellets, which are heavier than standard lead beads, pattern densely in many shotguns. Tests show they provide awesome knockdown power and penetration to anchor gobblers out to 35 yards and beyond.

Should you use No. 4, 5 or 6 shot for toms? I'm a No. 4 man, but most of the pros I know, including Michael Waddell, prefer 5s or 6s. However, it really doesn't matter. Purchase four or five different loads with various shot sizes. Hit the range; set turkey targets at 20, 30 and 40 yards, and test those loads through a couple of super-full and aftermarket choke tubes. Then go out and smoke a turkey with the load that patterns best in your gun.

Stake decoys 20 to 30 yards from your set-up tree. If a gobbler struts alongside the fakes, you know he's in shotgun range.

Aim True

One April morning a buddy and I worked an old gobbler for over an hour. The bird finally fell for our love yelps and waddled in. "Take him," I hissed. Steve settled in for the shot, but when his 12-gauge roared, I noticed his head was a good six inches off the stock. He missed. "I can't believe I did that," whined my friend, who has shot a bunch of turkeys over the years.

"Man, it happens all the time," I answered. "You just pulled your head."

That didn't make Steve feel better at the time, but it illustrates a critical point. Many turkeys keep their beards and spurs each spring because hunters fail to keep their heads down on their gun stocks. If you raise your head and look at a gobbler while you press the trigger, you'll probably blow it and pull the shot high.

When a gobbler is close and raises his warty periscope, drop your head and cheek your shotgun. Snuggle low and really dig into that stock! You're almost ready to pull the trigger, but remember one more not-so-minor detail—aim! In the heat of battle, when a big tom explodes into strut or runs out his neck and gobbles 20 or 30 steps away, it's easy to get flustered and shoot at a whole bird instead of a small spot on his neck.

When a tom is inside 35 yards, pin the barrel bead (or a scope's crosshair) on top of the major caruncles, those red, fleshy globs that rim a bird's neck like cheap costume jewelry. "I don't like to take longer shots, but when I have to, I aim a little higher," adds Waddell.

The Georgia pro explains that at 35 or 40 yards and beyond, a shot pattern begins to open up big time. "On a long shot, I want to hit a turkey with the middle and bottom of the pattern, so I aim for the top of his head. You never want to body-shoot a gobbler with the bottom of a pattern. You'll miss the turkey or, worse, wound him."

Once your aim is true, slip off the shotgun's safety and squeeze the trigger. Don't yank the trigger or you might pull the shot and miss.

Summary

You've set up in a good spot and panned with the gobbles, drums and footsteps of a tom as he marches in. He pops into sight 30 yards away. Take a deep breath and chill. Lean a few inches left or right to take a sapling or limb of out play. Cheek your shotgun, aim at the bird's neck vitals, slip off the safety and squeeze the trigger.

Boom, you got him! With a shooting plan like that, you might never miss a turkey again.

Bowhunting FAQs

with Jay Gregory

Pro Jay Gregory has bowhunting for turkeys down to a science, as his answers to these FAQs attest.

Many people think bagging a turkey with a bow and arrow is nigh on impossible. Just how difficult is it?

"Well, ten years ago I thought it was impossible too," says Gregory with a laugh. "I started out doing it like everybody else, basically using the same tactics that shotgun hunters use. I'd move in on a gobbler, set up in front of a big tree and call. When a gobbler came in, I'd try to wait for him to duck his head behind a tree or some brush. But when I tried to draw my bow and shoot, boy was that tough! A lot of turkeys would see me and spook. If two birds came in together, it was almost impossible to get off a shot. I called in a lot of gobblers, but wasn't very successful getting them."

After a decade of trial and error, Gregory bagged the traditional setups. "Now we bowhunt from blinds and always use decoys," says the Missouri pro. "The way we do it, turkeys never see us, and getting good shots at them is not all that tough."

Which bow, arrow and broadhead are best for turkey hunting?

"I use my deer-hunting bow, but I back the draw weight down to 60 pounds or so for turkeys," says Gregory. "If I need to, I can draw and hold awhile for a gobbler to turn just right for the shot."

Most of the time the pro uses the same arrows for both bucks and toms. "Sometimes I'll go with a shaft that is a little lighter and flatter-shooting for turkeys," he notes. "But it's no big deal, because most of my shots are short, ten yards or less." Either aluminum or carbon arrows work fine.

Years ago Gregory used a fixed-blade broadhead for turkeys. No more. "You can't beat an expandable head with a two-inch cutting diameter. You would not believe the damage that thing does when it hits feathers and bones. The arrow may or may not pass completely through the turkey; either way, the turkey usually doesn't go far."

Zapped solidly with an arrow and a mechanical head, a turkey might run 50 or 60 yards. "Other times a gobbler will go down hard, right in the decoys," adds the pro.

What other gear does a bowhunter need?

"I highly recommend a camo blind," says Gregory. "These days we do all our hunting and filming out of a Double Bull Blind. It has a roof and windows and hides you to the max. It weighs less than ten pounds and is

The Expert: **Jay Gregory** of Cameron, Missouri, is an awesome bowhunter—not just for deer, but for wild turkeys as well. Each spring Gregory and his friends hunt in five or six states and arrow five or ten longbeards, on videotape no less. That's five or ten more turkeys than you or I might ever get using standard archery tactics! Since 1990 Gregory, host of *The Wild Outdoors* television show, has tweaked and refined his technique.

easy to pack. A cameraman and I can go to a gobbler, set up the blind and be calling to the bird in less than a minute."

To sit comfortably in a blind and to set up a good sitting shot at a turkey, use a small stool or seat. You also need a bow holder that sticks into the ground and positions your bow close beside you. That way your hands are free to use a call or dig stuff out of your vest.

What turkey calls do you use?

"I use a variety of mouth and friction calls, but my favorite is the push-peg," says Gregory. "I am by no means an expert caller, but I can get the job done with that little call."

The Missouri pro has a cool routine. He holds the push-peg up to the front window of his blind and clucks and yelps. He then holds the call off to either side of his body and behind him and yelps some more. "The blind muffles the calls, and by moving around my clucks and yelps, I try to sound like a hen playing hard to get and moving away in the brush. Sometimes that really helps to bring in an old gobbler."

What are your best hunting tactics?

"I like to hunt back in the timber early in the season," says Gregory. "A lot of the time that is when birds are fired up and gobbling well, but they don't have hens yet. They'll mill around in the timber and follow the hens to feeding areas."

The pro starts scouting in February and looks mostly for tracks and fresh scratchings. When the season opens, he moves into the woods and sets up his blind. If he doesn't get a gobbler at fly-down time at first light, he might ambush one later in the morning. "If several birds are gobbling in the timber, we might sit and wait for two or three hours," he says.

"Once turkeys fly down it sometimes takes them awhile to show up at a feeding area." Also, by sitting tight and calling in a blind, the pro doesn't wander around and spook a bunch of turkeys, and that ups his odds of success.

Later in the spring Gregory often bowhunts in and around fields, pastures or plains where gobblers strut for hens. He typically sets up along fencerows or edges, but he is not afraid to set his blind smack in the middle of a strutting area if he has to. "It's amazing," says the Missouri pro. "A deer will see a blind stuck out in a field and spook from 200 yards away. But a gobbler will often strut right up to our decoys, coming within mere feet of a blind, even when it's out in the wide open. Come to think of it, I've never seen a gobbler spook because of a blind. Hens are another story. Sometimes they get jittery, but not the gobblers."

Decoys are a big part of your success. How do you use them?

"We use the 'spring jealousy' concept I devised a few years ago," says Gregory. "It's pretty much changed the way we bowhunt turkeys."

At the core of spring jealousy is a two-piece stake with a spring in the middle. You stick a foam hen on the stake and then sit a fake jake smack on top of her. You clip safety pins to the tails of the decoys, and then attach fishing line or string. Working the string from a blind as you call, you create the illusion of a jake treading a hen. "That rocking motion seems to do the trick," notes Gregory. "It drives some gobblers wild."

The spring jealousy set works great in a field or other open area where toms come to strut. Set up your blind, climb inside and rock the decoys as you cluck, yelp and cutt. A longbeard might spot the spectacle from 100 yards or farther away. The old boy might do a double take, and then

QUICK TIP

❖❖❖❖❖❖❖

If you bowhunt turkeys the old way, outside a blind, try the double team. Move in on a gobbler and kneel in front of a large tree with a light screen of cover (make sure you have at least two good shooting lanes). If you shoot right-handed, try to set up where a bird will come in and pass through an opening 20 yards to your left (vice versa for southpaws). Have a buddy sit and call 40 to 50 yards behind you. A tom might strut in off to the side and look right past you as he homes in on the "hen" calling back in the brush. Wait for his head to duck behind a tree, then draw, aim, sling an arrow and hope for the best.

❖❖❖❖❖❖❖

waddle over to assert his dominance over the audacious "jake" that dares breed the "hen."

Half the toms that approach the spring jealousy set droop their wings, poke out their chests and beards, and strut round and round the decoys. "Many gobblers come in and rub up against the decoys, or try to knock the jake off the hen," notes Gregory. "It's quite a sight."

Here's the best part: When an old tom is transfixed on the fakes or trying to spur them, he won't give a flip about your blind. He'll never look through the hide's window and see you drawing your bow.

Gregory sets the spring jealousy about eight yards from his blind, angled out the front window where he can easily release an arrow. "Sometimes I set a single hen, a confidence decoy, three or four yards from the breeder pair, but that's not necessary," he says. "Ninety percent of the gobblers that come in walk right past the hen and lock in on the spring jealousy."

When bowhunting, using decoys is a key tactic for success.

Okay, so how do you make the shot when a gobbler struts in?

"I want an eight- to ten-yard shot at a turkey, so I set my decoys eight yards away," says the Missouri pro. "Most of the time, if you're patient and don't jump the gun, a gobbler—if he's hot—will wade into the decoys. But even if he hangs up a little ways off the breeder pair, he'll usually still close within 15 yards."

While the shotgunner fires at the head and neck of a turkey, the archer aims for the body vitals. "They're about the size of a softball," points out Gregory. "I'd probably never shoot at a gobbler past 30 yards, but with the way we hunt, we get closer shots."

The Missouri pro advises you to shoot either when a tom is quartering on or quartering away. "When a turkey is quartering toward you, aim just left or right of his beard. On a quartering-away shot, try to put an arrow in tight behind the wing."

For the archer, the ultimate challenge has always been when and how to draw without getting busted by a laser-eyed tom. But if you hunt from a blind and set your decoys just right, you won't have to worry about that anymore. "Wait for a gobbler to turn just right, and then draw your bow and release an arrow in one smooth motion," says Gregory. "If you hit the turkey well, he won't go far."

ONE CRAZY MORNING

One spring morning Jay Gregory and his cameraman slipped in on a Nebraska gobbler. "That bird was hot. He just gobbled and gobbled," recalls the pro. "I didn't have to call much—a few clucks and yelps were all it took. The turkey strutted in and I shot him at eight steps. He went right down in the decoys."

Just then another tom thundered behind the blind! The hunters looked at each other and grinned. "You can shoot this thing, right?" asked Gregory as he handed over his bow and grabbed the video camera.

"You bet," roared his pal, who had been practicing with the bow back at camp.

The hunters swiveled around and dropped the blind's rear window. The tom roared at their calls, but he strutted and circled just out of bow range. "Oh well, at least we've got one turkey," Gregory thought. Then another gobbler bellowed back in the decoys!

The hunters whirled back around and gasped. "A third gobbler strutted in, jumped on top of the bird I had shot and started treading it," Gregory says. The cameraman's shot was true, and a second longbeard piled up in the decoys.

"It was a crazy morning," says Gregory with a laugh. "Of course it rarely happens like that, but you never know when you're spring turkey hunting."

Index

Contributing Photographers

Jon Blumb
Lawrence, KS
© *Jon Blumb: pp. 11TL, 13, 31*

Kathy Butt
Portland, TN
© *Kathy Butt: p. 70*

Tim Christie
timchristie.com
© *Tim Christie: pp. 24, 26, 30, 52, 61*

Soc Clay
South Shore, KY
© *Soc Clay: pp. 22, 103*

Michael H. Francis
Billings, MT
© *Michael H. Francis: pp. 80, 93, 95*

John Hafner
Indiana, PA
© *John Hafner: p. 17*

Michael Hanback
Warrenton, VA
© *Michael Hanback: pp. 9, 11TR, 34,
109*

Brad Herndon
Brownstown, IN
© *Brad Herndon: back cover C, pp. 27,
32-33, 46, 60, 78, 99,102*
© *Carol Herndon: back cover TL, pp. 8,
10, 54*

Tes Randle Jolly
Tuskegee, AL
© *Tes Randle Jolly: pp. 21, 29, 40B, 44,
45, 48-49, 51, 56, 67, 70-71, 86, 97,
104 both, 105, 112*

Donald M. Jones
Troy, MT
© *Donald M. Jones: back cover B,
pp. 11CR, 12, 41, 43, 50, 62, 68, 74,
76-77, 81, 83, 90-91, 100, 108, 110,
114, 119*

Brian Kenney
North Port, FL
© *Brian Kenney: p. 19*

Gary Kramer
garykramer.net
© *Gary Kramer: cover, pp. 4, 55, 72, 94,
96*

Bill Marchel
billmarchel.com
© *Bill Marchel: pp. 11CL, 11BL, 11BR,
14, 64*

John E. Phillips
Birmingham, AL
© *John E. Phillips: p. 122*

Len Rue Jr.
Blairstown, NJ
© *Len Rue Jr.: p. 57*

Dusan Smetana
dusansmetana.com
© *Dusan Smetana: back cover T, pp. 6-7,
84, 87, 88, 107, 113, 118*

(NOTE: T=TOP, C=CENTER,
B=BOTTOM, L=LEFT,
R=RIGHT, I=INSET)